F*CK THE SLIDES

By Nir Zavaro

PASSIONPRENEUR®
PUBLISHING

F*CK THE SLIDES

By Nir Zavaro

F*ck the Slides
Copyright © 2023 Nir Zavaro
First published in 2023
Cover design: Tomer Zakai

Print: 978-1-76124-117-8
E-book: 978-1-76124-118-5

Because of the dynamic nature of the Internet, any web addresses or links contained in this book may have changed since publication and may no longer be valid. The information in this book is based on the author's experiences and opinions. The views expressed in this book are solely those of the author and do not necessarily reflect the views of the publisher; the publisher hereby disclaims any responsibility for them.

The author of this book does not dispense any form of medical, legal, financial, or technical advice either directly or indirectly. The intent of the author is solely to provide information of a general nature to help you in your quest for personal development and growth. In the event you use any of the information in this book, the author and the publisher assume no responsibility for your actions. If any form of expert assistance is required, the services of a competent professional should be sought.

Publishing information
Publishing and design facilitated by
Passionpreneur Publishing
A division of Passionpreneur Organization Pty Ltd
ABN: 48640637529

Melbourne, VIC | Australia
www.PassionpreneurPublishing.com

*The worst things that happen to us often turn out
to be the best stories we'll ever tell.*

*This book is dedicated to all those who have fallen,
gotten back up, and tried again.*

Table of Contents

Introduction

People started to gather around Brian, with almost everyone holding a pint of beer. There were probably a dozen of us on that cold St. Patrick's Day. After spending a few days with Brian and his family in their hometown of Dublin, it was apparent they had a unique relationship, and I, being just out of one, couldn't help but ask him how they had met.

"Ho, that's a good story," he replied.

Within ten short minutes, we were all in love with their love story. That night, I made a decision: I wanted to collect more stories. I believed we were all the same—people with good stories to tell—and I wanted to hear them, to meet people and help them craft those stories.

You could say my journey started there. Or perhaps you could say it started in March 2018 with a tour in Europe teaching entrepreneurs the art of storytelling. Or perhaps even in 2017, when I started working with startups. Then again, maybe it was in 2014, when I started to teach brand management at college. Or maybe even in 2010, when I started my agency.

It could even date back to my years working as a marketing and brand manager. Microcopy, copy, articles, news websites, blogs, ads—I have told almost every type of story in every possible form. But it took me two decades to get to a point where I clearly understood what I wanted to do. There are very few, very rare moments in life where you *know*, when you can feel it—when it all comes together. The hard work you've put in, the feeling of excitement and adrenaline, the overwhelming sense you have made it. If you have ever experienced that, it is the result of hard work—a big goal, a pinch of luck, and a whole lot of long hours put into your dream or passion.

I remember that feeling when I opened a successful club many years ago. Forty-eight hours before opening night, nothing was ready. The acoustic ceiling was still being built on the floor and the speakers hadn't arrived, but we knew, sitting there at 2 am, that this place would be magical, and it was. Those moments—they take a long time to materialize.

For me, I probably fell in love with storytelling and sales much earlier. As a young party promoter at the age of 13, it was less about the money and more about meeting people, building new connections, learning how things work, and embarking, unknowingly, on a life journey to meet as many people as possible.

I have long been driven by the desire to help companies succeed. I have no idea how much money I have helped individual companies raise—I have never kept tabs on it. Maybe I should have, seeing as that is the metric people like to flaunt as success, regardless of the actual help or value it added to their business practice. Telling stories has been a part of my life since I was a child. As a kid, my father would tell anyone willing to listen that he hoped I would find a job involving speaking because I would not shut up (this is still true today).

Well, thanks, Dad. I did.

But more than anything, I loved meeting people for coffee. I absorbed people's personalities and learned about different businesses, industries, and ways of thinking. Discussing, asking, arguing—as long as it was in a coffee shop, I always said yes. For hours and hours, days and years. In some places, the staff still know my name, and one of my favorites has a cup with my name on the shelf. And what did I do most of the time? You guessed it: I told stories.

As I keep traveling the world, country to country, I still am in awe of the fact that we humans are all the same. True, we look different, and the culture might vary, but basic interactions, non-verbal cues, and emotions are the same all over the world. And as such, we also have the ability to tell stories. Equally, we are capable of falling in love with the idea of learning and becoming better at it.

I am honored and excited to share my learnings with you in this book. No matter how you tell the story or where you pitch, this much-needed skill is the basis for everything that follows. It can be taught, you can be trained, and it is time you share your stories in a new way.

How to use this book

Most books are read once and put aside. This methodology is meant to be a practical way of honing your skill. While reading, try and take notes or mark the areas you understand; pay attention to the areas you are good at and those areas that require more practice. You can do the exercises right after each chapter, or you can read each chapter for a second time before you start those exercises.

Once you have a specific pitch to work on, please review each step from chapter six onwards. You can use the exercise explainer in each of those chapters, and if you are uncertain, you can go back to the beginning.

Artificial intelligence

Writing a book about storytelling without mentioning the AI revolution may imply that I am ignoring it. We live in such interesting times—being able to craft a good story is even more important than ever. True, we already ask AI to write our blog posts and design our pitch decks, but we have slowly stopped communicating with each other. We are passing information rather than creating connections—real, deep connections. We have implemented technology as if it will always be there to do the work with and for us, but just like PowerPoint slides have become a crutch in our presentations, similarly, we will become dependent on AI. Like losing weight, there are pills for that, but if we want to get into shape, we must put in the work and train. The same applies to storytelling. If we do not practice, we will not be able to craft a good story when it matters most.

Why curse?

No matter what I did, people reverted swiftly back to those slides. Drawing their attention, making them feel unease in their chairs, F*ck was not used lightly but to serve a purpose. Like the F word or not, the goal of the provocative title of this book is to stir something in the minds of people who hear it or see it on the shelf. And let me tell you, most people get it. Some have reacted by laughing and saying they love it. Some have said they must read it, while others have gone on a long rant about how much they agree. As much as I curse in real life, this book will try and avoid cursing—we have many more important things to do.

For me, a good title is always a great reason to write a book.

1

ANOTHER DEMO DAY

The room is packed. People are starting to take their seats; some are trying to grab another bite to eat, while others are still chatting. There are dozens of venture capital and angel investors; some representatives from major tech companies, familiar brands we use every day; and some journalists.

Another demo day, ten aspiring startups. This is their chance to shine in front of all these influential people. Each founder has three minutes to do their best, to wow the audience and turn the crowd into their newest fans. Each one is hoping for a good reaction, a potential meeting, or worst-case scenario, some feedback.

I have been to a few of these meetings; they always felt the same. If the CEO was good, or the product really hit a nerve with someone in the crowd, they were able to raise capital.

If not, you hoped the food buffet was nice. No one should sit through another boring presentation, and those who are presenting deserve the ability to do better. We must improve; we must rethink. The process of raising money is truly a unique occurrence but it has mostly stayed the same over the last two decades. It felt like everyone was doing the same thing just because that's how it has always been done. What if I could offer a different way of thinking, a way of thinking outside the box, of reimagining this box?

Having worked with semi-tech companies on small ideas that never matured into products, I wanted to tap into the startup nation's sense of opportunity. I also wanted to be part of the hype, and so, with zero knowledge, headfirst, high hopes and no ropes, I went for it.

I needed someone to hold the door open for me. Things progressed slowly until a friend reached out. She and her fellow founders thought they could use some assistance after joining an accelerator. We met for drinks at my bar, where I was introduced to the accelerator crew.

As luck would have it, the accelerator admin staff member used to be a hostess in one of my bars, and even though she was somewhat skeptical, she agreed to invite me to meet with the companies. By the end of our first evening together, they felt they had received more value from me than from most of their other mentors.

In total, I ended up with nine one-hour meetings over two days. Each company came in, and I was asked to aid them with their marketing and website and improve their product–market fit. It was clear I had to ask the right questions in order to get the most out of our one-hour sessions.

One company I met with had three founders—all with intimate knowledge of their company and its identity, right? Wrong. When I innocently asked what their company did, each gave me a wildly different answer. We spent most of that session redefining, rethinking, visualizing, and building what they actually did. Then the next company came in and stumbled over the exact same question. Not a single company out of the nine I met with could tell me what they do in one clear sentence.

I believed this was my superpower: helping founders understand what they do, how they do it, and how to turn it into marketing. We focused on their marketing strategy, their go-to-market, and some creative ideation. Success soon followed when more accelerators heard about my work and asked me to join. I began to work with dozens a month, mostly in one-hour sessions, and it was enough for most to get high value. In this industry, it's all about who you know, who you worked for, and who you have worked with.

Another demo day

As part of mentoring teams, I often got invited to demo days, and startups would reach out to hear my thoughts. During another one of those demo days, I realized I had just seen another batch, but none of them had really made me feel a sense of enthusiasm. They all felt the same. Same pitch, same structure, same vibe. It got me thinking.

Why do some people successfully raise capital with nothing but a good pitch, while others struggle even when they have a better product?

How is it that some people will raise money with a bad idea while others fail?

They all have the same tools: a chance to present, show slides, answer questions, and send some decks.

That's it? Really?

The feeling stuck with me for a few weeks until I met another batch of startups; we explored the usual marketing ideas, but I also started to ask about their pitches. To my surprise, most founders did exactly what my students in their first year would end up doing: they would design slides, work on some talking points, and go for it. Sure, I met some who spent the time writing their whole pitch, but these were often confusing, with most employing technical terms in a short presentation.

When asked if their presentation is ready, most founders I've met for the first time have replied with a hesitant "yes." Then they present, and it sucks. If only they had a story that was their own. If only they could create it by themselves. If only they could measure and improve it. I would often ask them if they would prefer to pitch for three minutes or write a five-hundred-word article. Most would say the first is too short, the second too long. in fact, they are roughly the same in terms of word count, just a matter of perception. And perceptions can be changed.

Struggling to find any consistency, I saw an opportunity and started to help them. I also took the time to work with some more prominent companies looking to raise capital, and I even met with some companies after they had raised funds. The more I met, the better it got. All of them focused on the slides and added the speech after, not before. Design before writing? It didn't sound right to me.

Speaking in public

The more founders I met, the clearer the differences between those who were better at pitching and everyone else. There was a distinction between those who dreaded pitching and those who loved the stage. The good pitchers had confidence and were noticeably better at telling stories.

However, most of the time, *both* came underprepared; they counted on the slides to save them, instead of a good, compelling story to hold the audience's attention. Although they all understood they needed to improve by working on their pitch, the story, and writing it all down, most felt they couldn't do it. They felt they just needed to get through the presentation, and that they knew what they were talking about.

I realized that most people aren't interested in public speaking; they are just regular people, speaking in public, hoping to get it over with, and get the desired outcome. And in fact, those are the individuals who must begin to think like professional public speakers.

From demo day to demo day, I realized that all the mentors in the world wouldn't be able to turn things around with one-hour sessions. What was needed was a method to help them build a good story, one they could measure and improve.

A method

My next step was creating some guidelines, a framework that founders could use to improve their pitch. It worked for some, but as frameworks usually do, it did, in some cases, cause more confusion. What people needed was not a vague notion of how it could be done but an exact method for doing it. It needed to be simple, clear, and fast to implement, but more than anything, it needed to become a habit, something useful they could use in everyday situations—a step-by-step guide to improving their presentations and helping them overcome their fear or lack of skill.

So, my mission was to start writing my thoughts, my way of thinking. The way I listen, digest information, perceive, evaluate, feel, imagine, write, and speak. I needed to take this skill, this art form of storytelling, figure out what this method could look like, and meet as many founders as I could. Slowly I started to turn ideas into a meeting structure, a ten-hour work plan to help founders develop a story. One by one, I crafted my abilities to turn their ideas and companies into three-minute short stories, and it worked. More companies started to raise money, and my methodology was coming along well; the book was being drafted piece by piece.

I, on the other hand, was getting frustrated. You see, I had to write their stories and work with them. Yes, the method was there in my head, but I still wasn't able to fully transfer everything to them.

Frustration can be a great tool for learning, both for teachers and students, so I stopped writing for them. I focused on repeating the process but letting *them* write their pitch. And let me tell you, it was hard, but as the months went by, everything started to take shape. The jargon, the focus, the buy-in from the clients—people began to enjoy learning how to do it. And we started winning, my clients and I; we won competitions and raised capital.

Strangers

To have a larger influence, I needed to figure out how to share my thoughts with as many people as possible around the world. I began offering workshops, teaching people from diverse businesses, how easily anyone can learn and apply this method. The next crucial component was proving that, while we nearly never know our audience, we know how to make them feel. We mistakenly feel we must know them well, yet when presenting in front of a room full of strangers, it's only an informed guess. Including the audience in our story is an important part of the process. F*ck the Slides was ready once this phase was complete.

We have helped people clean water and cut down pollution; we have helped animals and extended lifespans. All these companies will eventually make a difference. I am thrilled I get to say I have played a tiny part in their journey, their story. and now, play a tiny part in yours.

2

THE SKILL WE ALL NEED

Whether we notice or not, we are all storytellers. We all tell stories. All day long, in every interaction. And selling a good story is all about feelings, hence we are all in the selling-feelings business. It is the skill we use the most to communicate, yet it is the one we practice the least. We refer to storytelling as a soft skill, but it's not. It is a *must-have* skill.

It is the basis of everything we create and build. This ability to describe the world, to connect, to interact, to project our needs and feelings onto others makes all the difference in our success. We all understand it; we know it when we see it, and we do it every day, everywhere. Yet we are still not treating storytelling as the most important craft we need to hone. The world has become so visual. Instead of communicating with each other, we think we can show information, but what we really need is a good story.

Pitching vs presenting

When it comes to business, we often confuse pitching with presenting. We think the presentation *is* the pitch, and so we don't practice how we will tell the story, hook the listener, and deliver the punchline we need. Instead, we make pretty slides. It's time to pivot back to the art and science of storytelling. When we master that, the slides are just icing on an already amazing cake.

In this book, you will learn how to rethink the way you use your presentations, what to focus on, and why you have the ability to succeed. Presenting is such a zero-sum game; in most cases, you either succeed or fail. Meeting a client, raising capital for a startup or a competition, or even convincing your boss to approve a budget—we all pitch.

In this chapter, you will learn why we need to tell a story to get what we want.

They are hiding

Why is it that the success rate for businesses around the world is less than 30%? For startups, it is around 18%, and less than 4% will raise a second round, while less than 1% will go on to raise any capital.[1]

---

1   Howarth, J. (March, 2023). Startup Failure Rate Statistics. *Exploding Topics*. https://explodingtopics.com/blog/startup-failure-stats#startup-failure-rate-stats

Just like researchers when it comes to survivorship bias—a cognitive fallacy in which one focuses only on examples of successful individuals (the "survivors") rather than the group as a whole (including the "non-survivors")—most founders form incorrect conclusions by focusing on the wrong thing. A good example of survivorship bias is when people tell you to look at the slide decks of Uber and AirBnB, which are often referred to as success stories. The problem is that we have no idea whether their strategy worked or not, as we have no clue what was said during the meetings.

Founders tend to focus on the visuals, the slides, mimicking successful presentations—all the while missing the most important piece: the story. Most hide behind the slides, using them as an anchor while speaking, but if we take those slides away, they are lost. Most are not natural orators. Some do not like to present, while others might think they are good, but they all improvise the most crucial aspect—the pitch—simply because they do not know what or how to salvage it.

The fact is that when we tell the story, what is said impacts everything. Regardless of whether we have slides, when we pitch, *we* are the storytellers, so *we* are the presentation. Everything else is an addition or a distraction. But when our story is not written, when we wing it or improvise it, we have no idea how the audience will interpret what we have said. We, in fact, are not in control of the presentation. We just hope for the best. Almost everyone uses the same structure: an overdose of information, slide after slide, lacking any feelings or a reason to care about the audience's reactions. The only way to solve this lack of presentation skills is to hire a coach, which involves simply working on a specific pitch but not training on our most important skill: the story we tell.

We believe our audience will make logical decisions based on logical information. We give them the wrong input expecting the right output, and then we wonder why we don't get the results we're looking for. That is, we assume the audience wants only logic, but first they need a connection, and that is completely emotional. Only once we have established that connection can we make the logical, well, feel *logical*.

And then we call everything a presentation, or a deck, or a pitch deck, using the same words to describe different things, leaving the elevator pitch as a barely spoken attempt to share what we do. We forget that commitment, focus, and written and spoken words are key elements to help our audience not only imagine but understand our story and join us on our journey.

Therefore, when I asked the founders to put the slides aside and focus on writing the pitch in an interesting way, they were not able to do that. It proved quite tough. Most reverted back to bullet points on slides. But the problem was not the slides—it was their lack of ability to create a story, let alone define and measure what is good.

AHA

When I realized that storytelling was the key, it was clear the slides were in the way. The only fix possible? Take the slides away. What are you left with when you take the slides away?

The story. *Your* story.

It was time to create a new way of pitching, but more than just preparing a pitch, we needed something that could be taught and duplicated: a successful method to communicate ideas and get the desired outcome.

Using the startup's demo day structure, which is a time frame to give a three- to five-minute pitch to ask for millions, I set out to create a step-by-step method for anyone looking to pitch. Unlike the usual pitch, which involves cramming as much information in as possible and hoping something sticks, I chose to go from the classic problem to solution by examining how people behave and how stories are received. We become obsessed with what we show instead of what we say. I realized that we must tell a story, but to do this, we must shift our focus from what we show to what we say and, most importantly, what our listeners understand.

What we needed was a way to ensure the audience gets the message, making them see what we see and getting them onboard. I was helping instill confidence in the presenters, helping them improve their ability to measure how well their story could resonate, tapping into the audience's brain.

All of this became clearer with time. The founders were able to duplicate the method and improve. Defining everything from scratch and turning the presentations from information-based to emotion-based helped the presenters understand the "why." They should be writing everything down, or at least stop improvising the most important piece of the puzzle: what they say. Learning this could work for almost every pitch. This meant it had to be implemented in a simple way, a methodology everyone could learn and repeat. A new way of becoming a better storyteller. So, f*ck the slides. Let's tell a compelling story.

And it works

You are the only one who knows more than anyone about your business, and therefore you are eager to show your knowledge and expertise. Once you understand how to story-wrap what you want to say—that is, take complex ideas and information and wrap them with a story the audience will love to listen to—it will forever be part of your process, helping your audience identify and join your cause. We will not change your idea or business plan—you can keep your pricing and market research, even the founders. The only thing we are about to change is the way you will tell your story and your understanding of how to structure and measure the pitch. I have worked with hundreds of founders, enabling them to achieve clarity. For people who achieved clarity, I was able to take them to the next level faster. Many would go on to become great presenters once they learned how to repeat the process without me.

Here's a real story. A company I worked with won a pitch competition in Singapore and finally raised money after achieving clarity and telling their story. They had spent almost two years before that struggling to explain their product and not raising a dime.

In another instance, a founder was referred to me by his initial investors. The company was successful, and growing, and needed another round of funding. He did not want to work on his pitch; he loved his product and believed it would be easy to raise money. After some months of failed meetings, he asked to meet me, and we nailed the pitch using this method.

After we went through the process, he had the opportunity for a Zoom prospective investor meeting. Using some of the techniques at the end of this book, he decided to build the slides anyway for his call.

Two minutes into his zoom pitch, a prospective investor politely interrupted him because he had started his pitch but hadn't shared his screen. He paused for a moment, thanked the investor, and continued his presentation without the slides, even though he had them ready to go. The story carried the pitch. He didn't need the slides. At the end of the call, everyone thanked him and told him they would be in touch.

About six weeks later, he called me. They had closed a $5.2 million second round of funding with some leading investors who were on the call without slides. F*ck the slides.

Who else has this method helped? An online E-commerce company, a payment service, water purification systems, a beehive platform, sports technology— hundreds of companies, including some in your industry. The list goes on and on, and this method will work for you too. It is simple to implement regardless of the industry or the state of the company.

Follow the path

Success is never easy. Learning a craft requires patience, much training, and a good guide. F*ck the Slides is a methodology created for those who are willing to learn, who understand that it is important to try things differently—those ready to put in the work. Many people ask me how I can create a pitch so quickly or help them craft their own story. To be honest, I have been crafting my art for over 20 years, and still, to this day, I go back to the basics and start again. To maximize the use of this method, we have to do a couple of things. We first need to understand your ability as a storyteller and how you think you are communicating with the audience versus how you should interact with them from now on. Once you understand how you are communicating, we will focus on four key stages of the storytelling puzzle—COLLECT, CREATE,

DIVIDE, SHARE—and how each part of this puzzle can help you improve, time and time again.

1. Collect: Organizing applicable information

The first step is to be able to clearly articulate what it is we actually do. It's that one clear sentence that defines us ... but beware, all these big words, the buzzwords of the day—*machine learning* and *AI based on the blockchain with community-oriented deep tech*—they belong to the next part, where we define the "how" you do it, which could be about a paragraph long.

The next step is to put everything we know about our industry, our business, our product, into categories, which we will call "information buckets." From problems and solutions to market size and competition, we define types of buckets and fill them up. The main buckets are the same as the sections of your pitch. For a startup, these could be: market potential, competition, how we do it, opportunities, team, roadmap, the ask, and the thank you. There are also sub-buckets, like TAM (total addressable market), team, industry knowledge, etc. In each bucket, we prioritize the three most important things. The rest will either be used elsewhere, or they just won't be relevant anymore.

All this information is the basis for your "unfold list." This list will be the foundation for the story you tell, for the scenes of your story, and will help it "unfold" in a logical progression.

2. Create: Layering the story

A good story needs scenes, a strong ending, and, most of all, a short, concise hook—a story within a story. In a three-minute pitch, about 70 words or 30 seconds is enough to catch your audience's attention; a decent hook will ensure you do so.

The hook is the most important part of your pitch. When creating a hook or a short pitch, we will emphasize our best attributes and make a strong claim, thus leaving us two and a half minutes to prove it. This unique concept allows for a strong hook that can be used anywhere, and it should stand in its own right.

You can do it all in 10 lines. A good story has a tendency to unfold by itself, scene after scene. It's almost as if *it* will tell you what should happen next. Using the unfolding technique, we will add another seven to nine lines under the hook. Now our story has a hook and a structure.

The next step is to create the "scenes" of your story.

In the first step, we created our information buckets, which will help us to plant the best information in the right scenes and not just blindly dump information onto our audience based on a slide's title. *Each piece of information must serve the story. It must create a scene.*

Writing a story is always easier when the outline and information are already there, laid out for us, and we just need to focus on each paragraph separately. It is easier to write a 30–40-word paragraph based on the scene from the unfold list and the information you have selected.

Then, it's time to wrap it up!

Technically, given all the hard work you've already done, you should have most of your story written. Once your scenes have been written, all that is left to complete our trailer pitch draft is an ending to tie it all together. This is your opportunity to remind the audience what happens if they choose you.

When you feel your draft is ready, we can move to the next step: measuring everything we have done before final editing.

3. Divide: Measuring the output

Short, to the point, with a clear message—that is how each scene, each paragraph, should be measured. This third step is all about measuring what we have written and where we aim to reach, kind of like KPIs for stories.

Every paragraph needs to carry its weight, and the right number of words per paragraph will ensure balance. The word count helps you focus and put the emphasis where it's needed. Without it, you might talk about your competition or a minor feature instead of sharing your solution.

To complete your draft, you must consider two things: what you want your audience to understand and how you want them to feel when they hear your pitch.

4. Sharing our story

They say practice makes perfect. When you read your story out loud for the first time, you will be amazed at how it sounds—most people are. Suddenly you will understand what works for you, what flows, your speed, your pace, and your intonation. Read it over and over, and make sure you incorporate these into your speech, establishing your voice. When you feel comfortable and ready to go *without* slides, we can start discussing everything else.

If the story is the spine, you, the performing storyteller, are the body. It is time we set up the stage and add supporting actors and scenery—slides, or any other visual aids that might serve you.

There is a fundamental difference between a presentation where you pitch and every other type of presentation. There are different situations, from a demo day to a meeting to sending out a blurb about you and your company. In the sharing stage, we will review types of decks. Put simply, each one is a group of slides serving a different purpose. For instance, a deck that you will not be there to explain is what I fondly call the "toilet deck" (because people will read them alone). The

Babylon deck, your questions-and-answers deck, helps you navigate through any meeting and creates a killer blurb, which you can send out or use in casual small talk. These are the types of decks that you need to cover it all. Remember, though: your deck is simply a visual aid to use when presenting, not a crutch!

We can change the way we practice our pitch; we can learn how to add the story elements.

From a sales pitch to raising capital, sitting with friends, or convincing your next hire, F*ck the Slides will change the way you approach your audience because it is more than just writing. Your message will be measured. It will be felt. The methodology will apply when the length of the pitch needs to be longer or when there are no slides. It will help you measure, improve, build confidence, and control the outcome.

3

EVERYONE LOVES
A GOOD TRAILER

A story is a transaction between the storyteller and the audience. The currency we trade in is feelings, experiences, and information. Each story has a purpose—to entertain, to educate, and, in our case, to open the door to what will later become the sale. A presentation is meant to provide information, while a pitch is meant to sell, and we are creating a story that combines the two.

Perception

We believe that the more time we get in front of our audience, the greater our chances of success in selling our story. In fact, the more time we take to pitch, the higher our chances of failure become. Another assumption is that we should appeal to a wide audience, but it is a matter of perception; a shorter pitch is more likely to succeed, as it has just enough of the right stuff.

Countless meetings, and we all have been in them, require a long ten to fifteen minutes at the start to explain the issue. That's almost as long as a good, well-rehearsed TED talk. But, during a demo day, startups might get as little as three minutes. For most, that sounds too short, not enough. What can be said in such a tight time frame when you need to explain the problem, solution, product, roadmap, the ask, and the team?

You are probably running those three minutes now in your head against the last time you had to present something, and it seems impossible. But, if I were to offer you an article on a leading website, let's say 500 words to explain your idea, that sounds better, right? Well, this is just a matter of perception, as they are the same. When pitching for three minutes, you will need about 500 words, depending on speech speed. So, it is more than enough. Now it is a matter of making sure we write it down before we pitch.

Everyone loves a good trailer

I love going to the cinema. I'm obsessed with movies and TV series and will watch anything—the good, the bad, and the mind-numbing. As long as it's entertaining, I'm in. But sitting there at the movies with a soda and popcorn, just as the trailers start, that's a special feeling.

The cinema hall goes dark, and it's time for the trailers. And *that* is an art form: short, precise, revealing just enough for us to understand and crave more without giving too much away. In most cases, we already know what to expect. Drama, comedy, mystery—we know the drill. Still, once the trailer is over, we lean to the person next to us and tell them what we think. A good trailer will make us feel something, intrigue or laughter, and an urge to see that movie. Now look here, I did not commit; I just sat there and saw the trailer. I did not buy a ticket, nor did I make any promises. It was just good enough for me to say, "I want more."

Seeing a demo day is like watching trailers before the movie. One by one, the startups appear on stage, all playing by the same rules, focused on data instead of selling me the story. They look the same when, in fact, each one is unique. They pitch the same where they should shine.

The elevator pitch, the deck, we've met already. All these names need to change. Most never had a story aspect built into them. I agree that they had a structure, but we have all used the same one: the technical one. The aim was to dump enough information and hope something stuck, to get that crucial foot in the door and, hopefully, another meeting. These things, good as they might have been, ran their course; they served their purpose, and our brains got tired.

No more *deck, pitch, presentation, intro, slides,* or *PowerPoint.* From now on, we will call it *the trailer pitch.*

The trailer pitch structure is meant to guide you and show you how a good story could be created and measured, spiced with feelings, facts, and figures. It gets the job done, selling the audience on another meeting, a desire to take part.

Confidence

We have gotten so used to relying on slides, on improvising based on some bullet points, that we are stumbling in the dark to find the right words. We struggle to look at the faces of our audience, so it's no wonder many of us lack confidence when we speak. Building confidence is about you, helping you present better, and knowing how to build the order and the outline. It's about knowing that everything relies on the spine, the story, and the text.

Actually, the verbal element plays the smallest part when we present, yet it is the most important part. In his studies during the 1960s, Professor Mehrabian created the 7-38-55% communication rule, which, although often misused, reflects how much the person in front of you will trust and like what you are communicating to them. There are many issues regarding the studies—the way they were conducted, the fact that they were female-only participants, and the lack of any data on the impact on a bigger audience—but one thing is apparent: if most of our communication is non-verbal, we must create the verbal, as it will serve as our spine, holding our message, voice, tone, and physical gestures. It will give us confidence that we know what we want to say, but more than that, how the other side will receive it.

You are a storyteller

There is a difference between written and verbal stories, and you might claim you are neither a writer nor a storyteller. But if you allow yourself the chance to learn, the sky is the limit. One of the best things (and worst things) is understanding that there is no right or wrong, just what fits into the story—what serves the plot. I often joke that I can't sing and probably couldn't cut it as a supermodel, so writing and speaking are the closest I will get to being a rockstar. When writing novels, I can write whatever I want. When telling a story, I control everything. In that context, I'm God. True, I can write anything, but consistency, the right amount of information, avoiding any bullshit— these will create an interesting story, and one that, when told, will be felt just as I intended.

Conveying happiness, sadness, or excitement is easy because you know what they look like in facial expressions and body language, and even how they sound. The only way of pitching better is to commit to writing your story, the spine, what you actually say. Everything else—the 93% of non-verbal communication—will emerge from that story. The more you write, the better you get; the more you practice, the better the story will sound. Stop improvising!

And commitment to writing a pitch word for word is one of the presenter's biggest fears. Many of us believe that improvising allows us more wiggle room and control, or that giving away as much information as possible will win the audience over. The writing allows us to look at things again and again, to craft, change, and align everything in a way that we say and act exactly like we intended.

Habit: The couch potato

"I don't run. Not anymore, at least not since my army service, but ... hmm ... thank you for the invite," I replied politely over the online video call.

"We will not take no for an answer, and it is only 10 km, not the whole marathon. Besides, you have like four months to train."

This was an invitation to attend a conference in Athens. The topic was *creating habits*. I had just helped the Greek chapter sell 100 tickets, and their way of saying thank you was to make me run the streets of Athens?

There are some moments in life that become defining. For me, saying yes to the invitation meant things had to change. Challenge accepted.

From couch potato to 10 km in four months did not sound like an easy task, especially when it was July in Israel. In Tel Aviv, even an evening run in summer means 32 degrees, with the humidity averaging 70%. It is so bad that you wonder if you are wetter before or after your shower. I went from short intervals to my first kilometer and then to three and to five. Four months after my first day wearing those sneakers, I finished my 10 km in Athens, Greece. To this day, I still run a few times a week, summer *and* winter, sometimes 40 km a week—and I love it.

Even though I still run frequently, I doubt that I'll ever win first place in a marathon—probably not even the annual 10 km night race in my hometown. What actually happened was that I went from being a couch potato to being able to run 10 km, and so can you.

There are three crucial habits you should start implementing in your day-to-day work process: note-taking, visualization, and intuitive writing.

Note-taking

Note-taking is the easiest way to make sure you capture your thoughts without the need to remember anything. It is about intent, freedom to forget, and trying to remember information. It allows focus and creativity to flourish. It is almost addictive for me.

I was once asked during an interview about my novel-writing process, "How does the story come to life?" I replied that there are two steps for me personally. The first is when I notice I'm taking notes of anything and everything that might be relevant, no matter when or where, because I fear forgetting my thoughts. The second part is when I start organizing all the information into buckets. Each bucket might consist of anything from ideas and words to links and numbers—anything that might be useful at some point to get my message across. The amount of data could be truly overwhelming, but putting it into buckets, each with its own subject, separates the wheat from the chaff, the crucial points from those that only ruin the story. I believe that even creativity needs order to be free.

Visualize

You can imagine the future, the next meeting, the pitch. What will it look like? How will you feel afterwards? The ability to visualize helps turn an idea into something visible and, thus, gives an idea of how the reality might look. Just like a business comes to life from an idea, you can also dream about what will happen next in your story. The ability to visualize makes everything more tangible. You can talk about things you see. Imagine the steps, identify the problems and the solutions that might occur, and write them all down. Your mind has the ability to bring forth the next steps, so imagine and write down a step-by-step plan of what you should talk about and how you might behave or how the audience might react. This will help you plan for different scenarios.

Intuitive writing

If you only take one habit from this book, let it be intuitive writing. It is always one of the biggest highlights during my workshops, especially when people feel the power of writing without thinking—otherwise known as intuitive writing.

The concept is simply a way of tapping into your subconscious, writing for the sake of writing, and letting your mind truly wander. It can serve you well when you're facing a problem. The best way to start is using a pen and paper. When writer's block appears, pick up a pen and paper and let your creative mind run wild. Many will say they prefer the keyboard as they can type faster, but trust me on this, use a pen and paper. Our brains work differently when we write by hand. It is easier for us to let our brains run wild. I usually suggest starting with three minutes. This is long enough to allow the mind to free itself and let the constraints go. It is also short enough, as your hand will get tired the first few times. After all, we are not so used to writing by hand these days.

Pick a thought to get you started. It could be a problem or something you want to think about. Set the timer and start. Once you are writing, keep going. Forget about typos, logic, or mistakes. Just keep writing. Your mind will need the first minute to get adjusted and let go. Only when the time is up should you read what you have written and let it sink in. You can mark the important things. Process it all. You will likely find at least one or two things that stand out that you might not have thought of before. This is the beauty of intuitive writing: it gets you into a deeper state of flow, unblocks you, and often helps connect you to things that you hadn't thought of on a conscious level.

Words matter

Words matter. What we say matters. How we say it matters more. Words define worlds, and you define it all.

Though quite counter-intuitive to everything we have been taught, the spine, the base for everything, must be written first. Crafting your pitch requires hard work. There is no perfect pitch; there is always a way to improve by trying new ways to describe things, a better way to incorporate information and data. The more you practice, the better you will become—and the faster.

Creativity comes when we acquire out-of-the-box thinking, but it can be achieved only when we know what the box is. You can start thinking outside of the box when you choose the words that create your world.

Then you are ready to focus on your audience.

Exercise

Pick a thought—something bothering you, a problem you are facing. This will be our initial line of thought. Now, time yourself. You can start with three minutes and work up to five minutes.

Write that first thing and keep going. Forget about everything—the outside world, grammar, and punctuation. They do not matter. What is important is the constant train of thought. No matter what happens, do not stop. Let it flow, have fun, and keep going until your time is up.

Once your time is up, sit and read; highlight or underline the relevant words, phrases, and sentences. You will be surprised by what you can accomplish in just a few minutes. Let your mind wander. It takes about a minute for your conscious mind to let go, but let me tell you, it's worth it when you start to see creativity emerge from this practice.

4

THE AUDIENCE

We are creatures of patterns. We have a core psychological need to define things and create order out of chaos. We require structure to feel good, to feel safe, and to understand the world around us. We prefer a routine—habits. For example, habit and prior experience have dictated that we need a ten-slide structure to be able to anticipate what will be presented in front of us.

Stories are just the same. We need a well-structured narrative. Our stories can educate, entertain, and invite the audience to join our journey. But more than anything, the audience plays a big part in our story. How they perceive it, how they imagine it, what they feel about us and about what we have just shared—this all matters greatly.

What we say is different from what the audience understands. Most of us do not fall in love with data for the sake of it. Thus, we need the emotional to make sense of the rational. We have all done things that we shouldn't have because they felt like the right thing in the moment, even when we knew all the logical reasons we should not do it. Why? We told ourselves a story that made us feel things regardless of the data we were taking in from our surroundings.

A good story is entertainment, while a good pitch is all about helping the audience understand they have made the right decision. Along the way, the audience measures everything we say—whether they agree or disagree—just like your brain is processing everything said so far in this book.

Experience

Those few amazing storytellers, the natural salespeople, can sell with or without slides because they place the right information in front of their audience, giving them just enough to make them feel it and want it more. They let the audience search for the missing pieces to create intrigue and suspense.

You can be one of them.

Fill in the blanks

"Now, listen very carefully. I am about to tell you a story. But you need to listen carefully, as it might have quite a few details, OK? Really, it's important, and I don't want you to miss anything, as you will have to fill in the blanks."

I finish this sentence and look at the audience as if I am about to perform a dangerous magic trick. I take a long breath and say one sentence:

"A MAN WALKS INTO A BAR."

Silence. People are smiling, looking at each other, waiting for the rest of the story. I repeat the sentence and give the audience another few seconds to soak it all in: "A man walks into a bar. A story."

I then proceed to randomly pick people from the audience and ask each of them a question. We start with the man: What does he look like? What is he wearing?

Then we move to the bar. Is it packed or empty? And what type of bar is it? Is there music? Who is he coming to meet? Why?

Take a moment. Think and answer these questions.

I've done this exercise hundreds of times in over 30 countries to different audiences, from students, startups, and small business entrepreneurs to CEOs at the helm of big companies. Never have I gotten the same answers. *Never.* Different people fill the gaps in different ways based on their imagination and experience.

When telling your audience a short story, you can paint a picture, and the audience will fill in the blanks. They will do it from knowledge and experience. The story starts when a man walks into a bar. Most people will agree that the man probably woke up in the morning, brushed his teeth, and put on clothes before he left his place, right?

Brushing his teeth does not serve the plot, so we can leave it out. If there are too many details, the audience will lose interest. Too few details and their brains will try and fill in the gaps from their own experience.

It gets interesting when we start asking about the bar. Some will fill the gaps based on recent visits to a bar somewhere. Others will pick a music genre they love, and so on. Each person will fill in the blanks with their own ideas.

Your audience is smart. They can fill the gaps when needed. Unnecessary information slows the pace, making it harder for the audience to follow. We tend to believe everything is crucial, but most things can be taken out, and you'll find nothing has changed. Give your listeners just enough to stay alert and not too much, or you lose them.

Tip: What we don't tell is what creates interest. They imagine; they think; they don't know; they want to hear the rest. They want to know what they do not know. They want to know if what they think is true.

That is a good trailer.

When I told you the short story of *a man walks into a bar*, we went from how did he get here to what is important and finished with but why is he here? And you all guessed different things. That was your next unfolding scene.

Read between the lines

When my first novel came out, I was broke, and I spent most of my days riding a borrowed bicycle around town, meeting people and selling them a copy of my book. A few weeks and 498 copies later, I met a girl I knew on the street.

"I loved your book, especially the stories in that bar. I immediately recognized it. So cool."

I was surprised. True, I based those scenes on a famous bar but not the bar she mentioned. After a few attempts to explain, I gave up. There was no point in ruining the book for her. For the first time, I realized something very interesting. All she had was a book—white paper and black ink. What she saw was between the lines.

People imagined what they wanted to see. The more explicit I became, the less room was left for their imagination. People will imagine in between the lines. That's where imagination happens.

Let them fill in the gaps. When you hold a book in your hand, it has weight; you think it might hold a great epic tale about a group of friends or a love story. It could be about a great war, about history or the future. But it is all in your head. The book itself is just plain paper and black ink. Your mind has the ability to fill in the gaps, to imagine that dragon or burning tower. Books tell the tale of days gone by or a city we have never visited, but we can close our eyes and be there, smell the streets or the food that is being served.

Emotions and feelings

Stories are designed to trigger specific emotions and feelings. Good storytellers know when and how to trigger each of these. Many people believe that we are all different, but we are the same. We mistakenly think that cultural differences make us unique, but these can be learned quickly and adapted in each market.

Emotions are a universal thing; we are all wired the same way. Paul Ekman, an American psychologist and pioneer in the study of emotions, found in his work that we all have six basic emotions. These can be interpreted by others through our facial expressions and have been found all over the world, even within ancient cultures that were never exposed to the outside world before. These emotions are anger, disgust, fear, happiness, sadness, and surprise. We all know how they look and what they make us feel. Later, different theorists suggested that there are more than six, while others like Professor Robert Plutchik suggested a wider array of more complex emotions, which he referred to as "the wheel of emotions." Nevertheless, it all comes back to the original six at the core of it all.

While these emotions are physical behaviors meant to convey something, feelings are how the audience will interpret these emotions and decide what they think of them. We will refer to both as feelings in the chapters of the book that follow. When we ask how the presentation went, the answer is subjective because we honestly do not know. We said what we believed the audience wanted to hear, but we didn't manage the emotions we wanted to share with them. We improvised those, so how did it really go?

Having presented my methodology around the world in over 30 countries, I can share that although many places have different cultures and codes of conduct that may vary, the basic, fundamental way we behave stays the same and is biologically driven. This allows us to create stories based on these emotions, making sure we connect and giving us options not just to control the narrative but also to make sure each emotion sets a chain of reactions for our audience—where they fill the gap or find an experience from the past, one that might match that feeling. This is crucial to make sure they feel what we want them to feel, increasing our chances of getting the message across and strengthening the logic element of our pitch.

Logic

The last ingredient our audience needs to process in the decision-making phase is logic. Having a pitch that is based on emotions with no rational aspect to it won't stick. Once the dust settles, as much as the listeners like you, your performance, and your enthusiasm, they must make sense of it all.

Emotions create actions; logic will persuade us to act on them. They go hand in hand. It is when they meet that our story becomes more than a good pitch. It is here that the story opens the listeners to a new attitude, from waiting to be convinced to being eager to learn more. It is the right mix that creates the connection, but it is a delicate balance between having enough rational data and pouring every piece into the story, especially overcrowded slides.

The best sale is a no sale

When you put too much pressure on closing a sale, the other side feels it. When making an excellent offer, the other side might be interested in it as well.

Creating a connection is the primary goal of the trailer pitch, rather than making a sale. Stimulating interest is the second step, and the third is to attract the right people to join you on this journey.

Forget the straightforward, hard sale. concentrate on selling wisely by showcasing your achievements, abilities, and experience. You are not trying to sell to everyone; you are selling to those who understand, need, and want it. When presented with a good trailer, believe that your target audience is intelligent enough to do the heavy lifting for you and recognize the potential. It's all about opening the door rather than closing the deal.

Every pitch, no matter where it occurs, is an opportunity to create a long-term relationship.

Remember that the best sale is a no sale. There will be another day, another pitch, and another chance whether you succeed or fail. So, take all the stress out of the equation.

Exercise

We have seen the audience's ability to fill in the gaps. Now it is your turn to try it. Here are two sentences to practice. Read each example and add at least five pieces of information from your imagination:

1. The dragon was coming down towards the tower.
2. The ship was getting close to Antarctica.

Now write down three to five points related to your pitch. Explain each one in a sentence or two. Be sure to avoid information the audience can complete without you.

Chapter 4
Fill the gaps

Add five pieces of information to this story

Add five pieces of information to this story

5

THE WHAT AND HOW

The "what"

Before we deep dive into creating our story, we must address what is probably the most common question every founder faces: What do you do?

Although it is a straightforward question, it is also the toughest one to answer. It is usually the first encounter, written or verbal, with our audience. Yet it keeps proving to be one of the biggest challenges for companies: to clearly define their offer in a one-liner. In this chapter, we will learn why most companies use the wrong way of explaining what they do and how you can fix it.

Most will use features and technology, trying to explain how they solve the problem instead of what problem they aim to solve. Many founders struggle with this issue, which in turn creates confusion and lack of clarity, internally and externally.

While I was attending some of the biggest tech conferences over the last few years, I took up the habit of walking around the early-stage startup booths—those raising their first round. Walking amongst them, checking out their company signs that explain what they do. Some are clear, while others are so confusing that I feel compelled to ask questions to clear it up in my head.

Most give a long, boring explanation, while others repeat what is said on the sign. And this goes much further than the first-timers. I have met many companies that were successful after a couple of funding rounds. Some of them had a product, and yet the "what" was their Achilles heel. They can't agree between themselves, let alone write it down clearly. So they all do the same thing. Let me show you:

> *"We are an AI machine learning LMS, building the future of Blockchain fintech. Launching the next generation B2B NFT concept, revolutionizing the CMS using machine learning."*

"Machine learning," "AI," "blockchain," "app," "platform," or "marketplace" all explain how we solve the problem our audience is facing. But these are not inspiring or thought-provoking.

These are just technical terms, when in fact your audience needs to get it quickly and in a simple manner. Complicating it for them might result in a negative reaction.

A few companies I asked said things like *making dreams come true*, or *making the world a better place*, or *helping you become your better self.* These were thrown at me during meetings with a matchmaking app, a travel insurance startup, and a habit app. While these big claims might sound nice, and they might be a byproduct, they lack any substance and have nothing to do with your company or the solution you offer. It is not a clear explainer of what you do; it's not a tagline or a slogan. To be honest, I'm not even sure where you could use it.

Fear of commitment

Albert Einstein is famously quoted as saying, "If you can't explain it simply, you don't understand it well enough." Although there is no proof he really said this, it beautifully explains the problem most startups suffer from: the inability to share a clear one-line explanation of what they do. If you can't be clear, how can you expect others to understand?

There are many reasons why this happens; generally, it is because we tend to skip the things we find difficult—that is why we often design the slides before we write the story. We cut corners. But, just as a building requires plans or software require architecture, so does successful pitching require you to write your "what." Sadly, words often become an obstacle, leaving us with an unclear, vague, too-broad-to-define concept.

Some founders fear the commitment of making a decision they won't be able to take back. Others would rather stick their head in the code or product just to avoid dealing with clearly defining what they do. In the meantime, they must keep moving forward, so most will just skip it, leave it for later, or use what they have as a placeholder. Too often, a long, technical, unclear sentence that says very little becomes permanent.

This one-liner will not go away; it will not disappear. Addressing it as soon as possible will help us avoid costly mistakes. We might find ourselves with a huge gap between what we have created and where we aim to get. It is easier to build a sentence than to change a whole product and months of hard work. But it is harder to commit to one sentence when we are always second-guessing our decisions.

A clear way of looking at the "what" is to define exactly what we offer and to which audience and what's in it for them. Strip everything to the bare minimum. Forget the buzzwords—focus on your value. What will they get if they ask for more information? If they scroll? If they sign up?

Example: *We help companies increase revenue.* Here, the audience is not clear. Increasing revenue could mean an endless number of methods. It might even seem a little dodgy, saying *we can get you more money.*

We help startups get better leads for less money. This time, the audience is clear, the value is that they need leads and we know how to get them for less money.

This newfound clarity will help eliminate background noise. It will help deal with internal issues, from raising money and sales to brand identity and marketing. Externally, it will define who we cater for just as much as it will send the wrong audience away. We do not want everyone—we aim only for the right ones.

The next step is to elaborate on the "how" we achieve what we claim.

The "how"

With a strong "what" comes a strong "how."

You have caught their attention; they want to understand how you can do what you claim. If the "what" is the solution, the "how" is the way there.

They came to you for a solution. Although the platforms you might use have an impact on their decision, you are not selling them the technology first. You are selling them a solution to their problem before anything else. In the "what," you made your big claim, your promise—but that is only the attention grabber. The audience now understands what's in it for them.

Now you need to elaborate on how you can achieve your offer. Why should they keep listening or reading? How will you help them?

This step is meant to strengthen your offer—your value proposition. In this phase, we appeal to their common sense and show them you know how you will get them to the other side. Your "how" is a two- to three-sentence explainer that might include information like the type of devices your solution will operate on (desktop or an app). It might include infrastructure, like a blockchain, or whether it is a SAAS (software as a service) solution, like a marketplace or payment method. This is the step where we clarify how the audience interacts and uses your solution to achieve the result they are looking for. Do not be in a hurry to add too many buzzwords—make a list and ask yourself how each word could amplify your offer. Using artificial intelligence (AI) or machine learning (ML), crypto or blockchain—each needs to add something.

Taking the example from the previous section on the "what," here is a relevant "how":

Using our machine learning capabilities, we can offer a marketplace for leads other companies do not need, and our automated AI will create the messages, send cold emails, and help you turn them into clients.

Another example could be: *Using our crypto marketplace, gamers can mine tokens while playing and purchase in-app skins. The more they play, the more they earn.*

Creating the "what" and "how" is imperative before anything else. Clarity with these will give you the opportunity to find your target audience, get feedback, and even start talking to investors. A company must have these two things locked down. Without them, it is easy to get lost. Two quick ways of checking whether you have nailed them or not are offline interviews and an online landing page. Both can be done quickly and cheaply.

Offline—people

My favorite low-cost and high-quality way to test a company's definitions is a simple conversation. I prefer a meeting or at least seeing faces to get their reactions, as there is so much rich data in non-verbal reactions. When I get the chance, I present my idea, something I'm working on. I'm mainly looking for feedback and any questions they might ask.

Talking to real people is the quickest way to get honest feedback, as long as you can see their reactions and expressions. This is more about letting them absorb what you are saying and asking what they understand from your pitch. Share your idea with at least ten people, and if they ask you "how," you've got it right. Feedback is important. If they do not get it on the first run, or they don't understand, use the moment to ask them what they are not clear about.

It is important to pause. Let them speak; do not interrupt. You must give them time to expand on their answers. This is the easiest way to test and fix. All you need is an audience; you can use meetings, friends, hackathons, and strangers. There are three circles you should test: people that know you, people from your industry, and complete strangers.

Online

Apply these same rules to your website or landing page. When it comes to online messaging, the top of your website should clearly define what you do, and the next part of the site should elaborate on how you achieve it. A feature list or another paragraph should elaborate more on your story. And then, importantly, you should test it. A simple landing page could be an excellent way of measuring how well your message hits the spot. It will take the average person half a millisecond to decide if they like this website enough to keep scrolling or leave, so make sure the design is well executed (if you do not have a logo or brand colors just yet, don't worry about it, just make it look nice). You need to give them a good reason to sign up for your waiting list. You can measure a user's behavior with simple free tools; measure what they read and improve accordingly.

Combine the two feedback methods—online and offline—by sending your landing page to friends. Inform them what you are working on and see if they get it. Ask strangers to roast your landing page on different social platforms and communities online; you would be surprised how much feedback you can get for free. Yes, it takes a little bravery, but it's best to be brave with strangers than to test new material when you are pitching to those who you *need* to buy in to your product or project.

Focus equals speed

I have met companies valued at over a billion dollars (unicorn status) and have worked with companies from the idea phase, pre-seed, and beyond that had no clear "what" or "how." These are probably some of the hardest questions you will need to answer because focus is hard to achieve. More than what you will offer, this confronts your business with everything you are not. Both are important distinctions that your audience needs to understand.

When you ask startups who their target market is, many will reply with pride, "Everyone." The real answer should be, "We would love for everyone on planet Earth to know who we are and have relevant people also know what we do, but we want to talk to the ones that might become our clients or refer clients to us." It is essential to narrow your audience so you can save time and money and ask the right audience the right questions. Remember: focus equals speed.

Exercise

Write what you do in one sentence. You can use what you currently have on your site, or the sentence you use to explain your business to your friends. Circle every buzzword that might be a better fit in a sentence about *how* you do what you do.

Now, rewrite the sentence, trying to focus on the value, offer, or solution your users might be looking for. Here is a simple template: *My offer is doing X for Y audience.* Consider how general the words are. If your sentence is too vague, clarify; if it's too complicated, simplify.

Write the sentence one last time and make sure your offer can be clearly understood by the potential audience.

Chapter 5
What and How

What do you actually do?

Rewrite the sentence

If needed, write it again

How do you achieve that?

6

BUCKETS

When I ask founders what information they feel could be crucial for the success of their pitch, most say, "Everything. How do we know what to leave out? How can we be certain that we chose the right pieces of information?" In this part of the method, we will learn how to collect, divide, and organize everything. Choosing what goes in is just as important as choosing what should be left out.

A story

I was getting ready to leave my office; the weekend was just about to start, and I was ready for a well-deserved break from my computer screen. When the phone rang, I had a feeling my weekend would have to wait, and I was right. A close friend who was on his way to the airport had managed to get a last-minute meeting across the ocean with some investors over the weekend. He just needed me to review his deck and see if anything stood out. Maybe I would have some insights, he said.

"Send me everything you have—information, data—let me take a look, and I'll call you back in an hour," I said.

As I was getting back to my desk, the files started arriving. Over 11 pages of information were included in the email. No order, no priorities—just a huge pile, all dumped into some files. As I reviewed the deck, I noticed dozens were on key information points, each overshadowing the other. Yes, they all seemed important, but together, nothing stood out. We had to start filtering it all until we had a bucket full of the purest information: what was a must, what could help, and anything else.

A bucket might consist of ideas, words, links, and numbers—anything goes as long as it helps you find your way with the enormous amounts of knowledge you and your team have. Storytelling is about knowing every angle but deciding *which* angle is the most interesting and how it connects to the rest of the scenes.

Collecting and organizing your information is the first big step in your writing process, and there are two ways to approach the bucket phase. The first and most common is when you already have a deck. If you designed or created the layout, you have probably given your slides titles. You won't need those in the design phase, but they are a great way to create your initial bucket list. Another option might be grouping notes together while titling each group. This is a good method when facing notes that might be scattered all over. When I'm working, I might find myself in front of thousands of words—a mixture of notes, ideas, and thoughts. It's tedious work, but I take the first one, put it in a new bucket, and move on to the next. Pretty soon, I will have several lists, several buckets, each covering a different topic, from competition to market size, value proposition to budgets, roadmap to product. Just make sure you don't create too many buckets. Somewhere between six to ten buckets should be sufficient for your 500-word trailer pitch.

As the saying goes, a gun in the first act will fire in the third act. If not, why put it there in the first place?

Looking at your list of buckets and seeing them full might be overwhelming, but if you could only choose three pieces of information from each bucket—the most important ones—which ones would they be and why? Prioritize them. There are three types of information to organize. The first and most important is everything relevant to your trailer pitch. This will usually include the top two to three in each bucket. The ones that do not make it into the spoken story might be added to the supporting slide. The second type of information might be numbers three to five in your buckets, depending on how many you have used in your trailer pitch. This will include everything you might present after the trailer pitch, during the meeting, and in the Q&A phase. Many of these will belong in your Babylon deck, which I will elaborate on later in this book. The final type of information left is everything else—and, in all likelihood, it is not needed at all.

Now it is time to have a fresh look at everything our story might need to have in it. The last step in preparing our information will be the final shortlist. The top three of each bucket will go into one list. The order is irrelevant here; they can be chosen from as needed for each paragraph. The story will dictate what information needs to be shared as it unfolds. This is the complete opposite to adding information under a slide title, where we talk about one subject and never return to it. Spreading information throughout the story where it is needed helps create a flow while strengthening the points you aim to convey.

It took us a total of ten hours from that Thursday call until my friend had to pitch. We knew two things: he might not have the chance to use his slides, and the people he would meet knew very little about his company. We went with a 30-second hook showcasing that he was a veteran, that his company was profitable, and that he had the right licenses and pipeline to scale. He ended up raising money from those meetings.

Being able to choose the right pieces of the puzzle and knowing how to access the right information without overwhelming your audience will serve you every time you start a story. We can always revisit and update our buckets and shortlist if we have new information. Remember, one piece should push out another in the final shortlist, otherwise you might overpopulate your story and clutter it. In the chapters that follow, when we start creating the hook and scenes, we will use the shortlist to populate them.

Exercise

Create a list of five bucket titles.

For this exercise, pick a bucket and fill it with at least six lines of information. If you chose market potential, you might add the total addressable market (TAM), type of users, total budget, and a couple more lines.

Now, review your list and decide the importance in descending order from one as most important. The top three should be crucial for the success of your story. Mark which one should be spoken or written or both.

Complete the other buckets until you have about 20 pieces of information ready to be added into your trailer pitch.

Chapter 6
Buckets

Add five bucket titles

Your chosen bucket for
this exercise is:

According to your chosen bucket, add your information here

7

HOOK

The hook is where the story starts. The hook is where we invite our audience to pay attention, where we grab them and pull them into our world.

In this step, we will discuss a new way of picking a hook layout and adding the information while ensuring it adds interest every time. Deciding where to start is probably one of the hardest decisions when creating a pitch. We should start at the beginning, but how do we know where our story really starts? The biggest obstacle we must overcome is our audience's judgement. Even when they do not say it, they are looking to be entertained and introduced to something new.

While most founders tend to start the same way—*here's a problem and a solution*—I am suggesting a completely different approach: take the listener from doubt to intrigue in the first 30 seconds. This is your hook. The audience is sitting with their hands crossed, metaphorically, waiting for you to convince them. Make people go from "convince me" mode to leaning forward and going into "tell me more" mode. Instead of building up the solution, explain what the final result might look like and use the rest of the time to build up your case, proving what you claimed when you started—prove your hook.

You see, whether we want to or not, we have become more skeptical than ever. With so much content out there and so many startups pitching, it feels like we have seen it all, and the burden of proof lies on you and your story. But we can change that—we can make the audience work to figure it out by creating a scarcity mindset.

Like a magician explaining what is about to happen, the audience struggles to believe, but when the magic occurs, they are dying to know how it happened. This is the hook we aim for: moving their mindset from cautious and skeptical to intrigued and interested. The goal is to get them to start thinking, *Wait, maybe we need to explore this.*

A story within a story. Our hook is based on making a big claim—where we are, how we have already solved it—then getting straight to the point in about 30 seconds. On average, we will use between two and four pieces of information to support our message. One of my favorite examples goes like this:

I remember the call. I was just at a football match during the world cup. It was about to start when my partners called me and told me, "We got it! We got the license to launch our investment platform!" People told us it would take forever, it's too hard, it's too complicated, but we believed, and there we were—four years later with 50 investments in our portfolio.

This simple 68-word hook was used in both meeting rooms and casual conversations. The aim here was to show success, experience, and track record. It created intrigue and interest, switching from doubt or waiting to be convinced to *maybe this is an opportunity worth listening to.* They raised money and have since launched in the USA.

Make a claim fast; flip the thinking from *what's in it for me* to *maybe this is something we should explore.* In a longer pitch, about 15% of the time should be spent on the hook, and for the rest of your time, you can enjoy proving your points with data and examples. There is one important thing to remember: *Start strong.* In the examples that follow, we will review different versions of hooks to test.

Experience share—put them in the situation

Taking us back to an experience we've had ourselves will stir up certain feelings associated with that event. Some experiences and memories make us smile, and some make us sad, but we have all been through a lot in life—we can relate, and that is what's important. Once the audience can place themselves in the situation you describe to them, they will feel your message, and it will ensure you start strong by inviting them into your world.

We have experienced a problem firsthand, and we wanted to solve it for ourselves—a sick relative, an injured pet, something lost. It could be an everyday situation, like this hook:

Running into the kitchen, seeing my father lying there on the floor, blood pooling around his head. He seemed conscious, but he was just lying there so helpless. If only he could have called for help. What if we got there a few minutes too late?

This is a true story. You are probably now feeling compassionate or thinking about someone you love, maybe even one you have lost.

Most of us know the feeling of standing next to the baggage conveyor belt, waiting, seeing everyone else picking up their luggage, noticing that there are just a few bags left unclaimed and wondering, hoping they have not lost your suitcase. And the belt goes round and round.

That was how we started a demo-day pitch with a start-up working on solving the lost luggage problem at airports around the world. Most of the people in the room nodded. They all felt it.

These are emotional triggers. They work much better than numbers; people feel them physically.

The case study/customer story hook

A customer story is straightforward. It goes straight to the intrigue. In 60–70 words, we need to tell it all: what happened, what was needed, how your customer dealt with the situation using your solution, and the happy result. This is what I like to refer to as the "I got it" hook.

In 30 seconds, the audience knows everything they need to know about the industry and the stage of your product. This will establish a context for your solution and allow you to elaborate on each point to make your case during the remaining time.

When working with a company in the fintech industry, we told the problem with a story about a last-minute global payroll problem. We all know what it means to get paid. Here's the hook:

A company had just acquired another international company, saving it from bankruptcy. During that phase, the company's assets were frozen, including their bank accounts, which meant they could not pay their 300-plus employees and vendors around Europe. Our solution enabled them to open virtual bank accounts in several currencies, and within 72 hours, they made all 300 payments in seven different currencies.

Give them the conflict—what failing might have looked like—and the solution to the case—*this client had a problem; using our company, they were able to solve that problem in this amount of time, saving that amount of money, and this is exactly what we do*—in one sentence.

A case study allows you to explain how you do it within 30 seconds, allowing people to just get it. It is an establishing shot that will build all other scenes and slides.

Write down a list of customer stories. Choose the flow of events; be concise; and show a start, a conflict, a journey, a solution—how it was untangled using your help.

Tip: Using a case study will also fall under this section, but note that a use case usually refers to a sequence or explaining a process based on in-depth information and might complicate everything. You might go with the use case info and construct a whole trailer pitch start to finish, but you should avoid using a case study in your short opening hook as it might prove too complicated to start with.

Numbers hook

Every morning, I get a cup of coffee from the same place. It's a really good cup of coffee, and it costs $6. Some might say it's crazy expensive; others might think it's reasonable if the coffee is that good. Others might ask if there is a cheaper coffee close by that might be just as good. We can all discuss whether a $6 coffee is too expensive, but it would be impossible for us to discuss if a six-billion-dollar or an eight-billion-dollar market is big or small—because how can we even grasp such a number?

Let me give you a scenario:

In their quarterly meeting, a company was deciding on whether to add a research budget. When this happens, the board of directors will discuss and argue whether it should be 16 or 18 million dollars. When that vote is over, the next line on the agenda is a $4,000 yearly salary increase for the cleaners. Some argue it should be avoided, as when you take into consideration the total number of cleaners in the company, it would amount to about $50K a year. They have just argued about a million or two, but when it comes to $50K, they can measure it, they can feel it in their pocket.

We become blind to certain numbers, whether it's because we have heard them so many times or because we just can't grasp them. Similarly, investors who see presentations all day might hear ten companies pitching for a different market, each with a different size, so what we remember might be completely irrelevant. We might judge it just because we have compared it to another pitch.

For these reasons, it is important to treat numbers differently: we must consider what the audience expects to hear and the numbers they can relate with. Another important thing to note is how we present our numbers, whether it's a percentage, compared to another number, or a standalone figure. Numbers are subjective. Use them wisely.

A former client of mine had a great increase in client traction, but those new small business accounts just didn't move the needle when looking at their revenue graph. We decided to focus on showing the client growth potential thanks to a quick sales cycle. We took a relative disadvantage and turned it into the potential to conquer small businesses fast until we attain enough market share to move on to medium clients.

Using random strangers' hook

When using strangers to talk about something, you must make them relatable—for instance, if they are young, they represent something. We tend to introduce them and dismiss them instead of turning them into a power play. Compare them to your audience—even a small detail can suggest that it could be you once upon a time, or it could be your kids.

Meet Daisy and John. They are a young couple, students, and they are struggling to save money.

Showing the audience these two lovely young people will probably not create interest or empathy. Your audience is going through so many problems of their own that they simply don't care. A good way to connect with the audience is via emotions or by adding a time element.

Daisy and John are just starting their lives together. They're young and idealistic, but they are among the 67% of young people that will default on their home loan in the next few years. With your help, we can build something that will help people like Daisy and John pay their mortgage, avoid bankruptcy, and raise their kids without worrying.

They become representative of a whole generation. We have given them names. We have a general timeline. If you read it again, saying no to helping them says something about you, right? It is crucial to make them relatable. Help the audience connect to their struggle; make them feel they have the power to help these people or at least to truly relate to what they are going through.

Remember, using a third-party character in your pitch can work, but they need to stay with us for the whole journey. Most presenters use the third character as an opener only to abandon them. In some cases, the presenter might try and return to them at the end to create a false sense of closure, but this rarely results in a successful pitch.

Have a very good reason for using them, or it might feel like bad exploitation of a nice young couple!

About you—the personal hook

A personal hook is one of my favorites as it puts you in the middle of the story to describe how you found the problem. It shows the audience that you acted and found a solution. This hook creates good feelings about you as a person.

Introducing yourself through the hook is a powerful tool, as it is unique to you; it resonates, and people remember. There are several ways to go about it.

It happened to me–an athlete got injured while training. This could have been avoided if only the coach knew how to measure the stress level of the athlete's body. The injury started a chain of other injuries until he lost his career. The athlete started a company helping sports teams make well-educated decisions, reducing athletes' stress and injuries.

Or,

While spending time in an old folks' house, our founder noticed that most people are young at heart. They need a reason to wake up and are eager to keep learning. With years of training in the LMS (learning management system), he decided to build an online platform to help older people stay connected while meeting like-minded people their age.

This story is one of my favorites of all time, and it starts with a sleeping bag—specifically, three guys in the same sleeping bag:

As kids growing up, they did everything together. They even made a pact to stay together. They are committed for life. During their army service, they enlisted in the same unit. This picture was taken in the reserve, years after they finished their service.

We showed that picture and made the audience feel they wanted to be part of that gang in that sleeping bag. Because they knew this was a good bunch to bet on.

Tip: A personal hook can be followed by a "team" paragraph, as it feels natural to add people to your journey. Usually, it is disconnected from the pitch, but it will reinforce your nature and your management skills and explain that you are the right team to back. This can be a vital pre-frame, as humans need connection to other humans.

In executing this tip, bear this in mind—often, founders will introduce themselves first. My suggestion is that you leave the introduction of your team as a side mention or leave your name to the end. This makes it more memorable, and it becomes connected to the final part of your pitch.

The beginning is the audience's first encounter with your story. It is crucial because it defines how the audience perceives *you* rather than your project. It is your chance to control the short pitch—the first 60 to 70 words aimed at showing your abilities and your track record.

Here, you invite them in and give them a reason to stay. Make them want more.

This way of thinking will lead us in the next few chapters, where we will populate our story with information and ideas. Choose your use case, fill it with information, and draft it.

Bear in mind that a great hook takes time to craft. So, invest the time it needs. Work on finding the right frame and context to put it in. Remember, we are turning the hook from a bland opening line into a point of connection and impact that creates emotional buy-in from the audience.

Exercise

Choose one of the five hook frames from this chapter, taking time to consider which makes the most sense for your business.

Select two to four pieces of information that could show your achievements and help present your success or potential. Use sentences and words that could help the audience understand and connect. It is about helping them understand where you are.

Aim to create a 60–70-word hook.

Chapter 7
Create your hook

Type of hook you would like to lead your pitch with

Write relevant information - Success, potential, achievements

Your hook draft

8

POPULATING THE STORY

Have you ever seen a storyboard—something a TV writer would use to plan a show? On it, there are scenes, and within each scene are core details that move the plot forward. As we progress to the point where we get ready to craft our story (and yes, even put it on slides that you *won't need to rely on*, which is the whole point of this book), we need to think about these scenes, what they contain, and how they unfold.

The unfold technique

When working with slides, we add words, placeholders, titles, or subjects we would like to discuss without any connection between them. Don't do that.

Starting with the hook from the previous chapter, we can move to the next step, our outline—the list of scenes, if you will. I call it "the unfold list." Before throwing in the details, we will create a short list of sentences, each describing what we would like to tell our audience next. When I told you the short story of *a man walks into a bar,* we went from *how did he get there?* to *what is important?* and finished with *but why is he here?* And you all guessed different things. That was your next unfolding scene.

We were at my agency office late in the evening, working on a presentation for a client. My colleague and I decided to take a break and order some food. While we were waiting for the food, I asked one of my managers if he would consider himself a writer, if he thought he could write a success story about one of his clients. He was puzzled, as his job focused on paid social media advertising, and he was never asked to write. He said that he could try, "But how do you start?"

We chose a client, and I asked him to share a success story with me. He was quick to give me a general idea for the hook but had no idea where to go from there. I simply asked him to tell me what should come next in one sentence. He replied. I smiled and said: "And?"

We repeated the process a few times, and there it was, all written on the whiteboard. We worked on the hook, and the story unfolded. He smiled. He was shocked. The next day, he submitted a 500-word success story.

A man walks into a bar. He is meeting his friend, but ... these words—*and, but, therefore*—have different ways of connecting the scenes. When pitching, the unfold list could use all of them, so be mindful of which one you choose.

The creators of *South Park*, Matt Stone and Trey Parker, have often shared how they learned to use **but,** and, **and therefore** instead of a general sentence or a full stop to move the plot from scene to scene. One way made the scenes seem disconnected. The other created continuity and caused the audience to look for what the connection might be. This might be put to good use when you want to show a problem and how you solved it. Keep that in mind, but don't overdo it. Stay focused on the logical way your story will advance.

Write a love story

I'm a sucker for a good love story. While working on the last third of my first novel, I really started to dive into creating the whole plot line. I knew what would happen—why the characters did something—so adding *but* and *therefore* made sense. I love it so much. In my workshops, we regularly write love stories:

Boy meets girl. Boy asks girl out. They fall in love. Girl has a dark secret. Girl hides her secret. Boy finds out. Boy leaves girl. Girl is heartbroken. Boy meets girl years later. They never stopped loving each other. They live happily ever after.

And now with the connectors:

Boy meets girl, and Boy asks her out. They fall in love, but Girl has a dark secret, and therefore she decides to hide it. But then Boy finds out she is hiding something and he can't let it go. Therefore, Girl decides to tell Boy her secret as he promises it won't change anything. After hearing her secret Boy leaves girl anyway. And Girl is heartbroken and keeps hoping they would make up, but he travels far away. Years later Boy meets girl. They never stopped loving each other but now Boy has a dark secret. They live happily ever after with one secret, and she never asks him about it.

Read the first story again. There is no timeline until *years later*. We do not know how long the first part took. We do not know what happened in between or what her secret is. We only have an outline and a list of scenes explaining how our story will unfold.

Start writing some lines about each of the key points you want to cover. It could be a short story, a few chapters, or a whole book. I write each of these on a separate line and take a step back. This is the essence of our story; the plot is there. People tend to think you need to write exactly what you plan to show, but in fact, starting small is easier.

Look at your lines, read them out loud and start moving them around any way you feel like. If a different line should come first, or if you feel you need to add a few words to better explain what you mean, make the change. It is much easier to move a short line around until it makes sense.

The unfold technique will help you spot anything that doesn't make sense. The hook will serve like the locomotive, dragging the story like a train; each piece is connected to the previous and the next. *He won't leave her if he never finds out about her dark secret.* Every line should support your claim, strengthening your initial hook.

When you feel the plot line is solid and that you have explained the general idea step by step, you can move forward. When written properly, it will make sense. It will simplify everything. A common mistake when starting purely from the slides is that of creating misconnections—a non-story where each slide feels like a new start.

Connect everything.

Powergraphs

The hook and your unfold list will serve as your anchors. For a three-minute pitch, I would suggest aiming for about seven or eight plot lines, which will serve as paragraphs. A general rule of thumb could be 30–40 words; in longer presentations of five minutes, aim for 60–70 words per paragraph.

Tip: They might vary in length, but they will each serve a purpose. Sometimes you will decide to arrange the paragraphs differently after the story is done, but that is normal.

The next phase will be to populate the plot lines, turning them into a paragraph with relevant information taken from the buckets. The easiest way is to take the top two ideas from each bucket and create a new list. The list no longer has anything to do with the bucket titles we had; these are now just pieces of information that need to fit our plot.

Using no more than two bucket points per paragraph, start outlining your story. Now, read your anchors and what you planted in each of them and get a sense of the story at hand. Anything that feels misplaced should come out. You can decide whether it should be moved to another place in the story or go back to the main list it came from.

If done right, if every bucket point becomes a sentence; our blank canvas is not blank anymore. Your story is almost done. You have a hook, a structure with your plot, and the information in each part. If done right, you should also notice that you already have about 30 words per paragraph.

It might sound difficult and complicated, but just like any skill we aim to acquire, we need to practice until we get the hang of it. Just get started and see your story unfold and it will become easier the more you exercise.

Finishing strong

Our trailer ending should leave intrigue and excitement, evoking the desire to know more and the fear of missing out. Your ending is a powerful opportunity to transition the hard lifting from yourself and pass the work to the audience. There are two types of endings you can look at, both with the same goal: making them choose you over others. You have told them everything they need to know, circling back to the essence of what you aim to achieve; now is the last chance to make them ask for more. Everyone wants to bet on the right horse, the winner, the company that will 10X their profit. We have the same feeling when we choose a competition winner or a vendor. We will leave our audience thinking, *Is it really that good? Will it be worth it?*

A sales trick would be to choose one of two ending types: the rhetorical or the transformational.

What would it mean if I said no?—the rhetorical.

What would it mean if I said yes?—the transformational.

Creating a rhetorical question for your ending is based on a strong value proposition. The potential should sound greater than the risk. Inviting people to invest in your company might mean saving the planet while earning, so not joining might seem like an illogical decision. If your offer sounds like this: "Give me a hundred dollars. If we succeed, we will give you back one thousand dollars." Create a strong value proposition—so strong they must at least keep exploring the option before they refuse. Let them take the risk and calculate whether they are willing to take the risk of skipping out on something good.

The second type of ending is an inspirational one: We want to change the world. If they only decide to go with one company this year, it should be you because, together, you can reshape how elderly people are treated; you can save the climate or help kids see again. It is not about overselling the idea but, rather, delivering the trailer pitch with a call to join your vision, inviting them to embark on this journey to make a big impact together.

If they could only choose one, why should they choose you? What makes you stand out? What can a strong ending do for you?

Exercise

Let's create your first unfold list. Read your hook, and just like in Chapter 3, visualize what will happen next. What follows the hook? And then? What happens next?

Keep asking the questions that leads to the unfold step-by-step.

Once you have several "plot points" on your list, write up the next few scene descriptions. Keep it to one sentence outline for each scene in a list, one after the other.

Chapter 8
Unfold your story

Your hook

Add your plot points here

+

+

+

9

WRITING AND EDITING

Knowing what you want to say is half of the creation process. Writing is putting it all into words, and editing it is crafting your work of art and taking it from good to great—from data to a single idea in each paragraph. By now, you should already have a few hundred words written. This chapter will help you craft them into well-organized paragraphs that work together to turn boring facts and numbers into one coherent story—one that could resonate.

You have taken the hardest part, the writing part, out of the equation by developing your hook, bucketing your ideas, and putting them all into a story. Now you can focus more on editing and crafting each paragraph.

While editing sounds like a gruesome process, I love it. It takes a rough draft and makes it a work of art. We will focus on trimming, connecting, simplifying, flowing, and having a strong finish.

Sculpt

We start with each paragraph. As the length might vary, a paragraph needs to be just as long as it needs to be to express the main idea. Words are expensive real estate in our pitch. Every word counts—literally.

The essence might take a few tries to really materialize, so do not worry about the length; rather, focus on the message. It is easier to write three sentences than a complete story. Review the full paragraph. First, focus on the key message, ensuring it is clearly articulated. Then, visit each sentence: What purpose does it serve? Is it clear? Could you use less words, or do you need to add something to clarify?

In this phase, we are not adding more information but pilling off excess; this is all about trimming. Restructure each sentence, add only must-have words. Read the whole paragraph over and over, getting the feel, the flow of it.

Connect

In movie editing, a jump cut occurs when a sequence of the same shot and the same character has suddenly changed, confusing the audience and making them aware of a problem or a plot twist. In movies, it could be used to call something out. But most of the time, it will be a mistake, a glitch, like the actors wearing shoes and, in the next shot, only socks. We want to make sure each paragraph in our story has the right flow, avoiding confusion with our audience. This might happen between paragraphs. The last sentence of each paragraph and the first of the next paragraph should feel natural. Read the two as a pair, making sure they make sense together.

Avoid repeating the same words, and if the last sentence ends on a high note, the next can't be low key. It must flow naturally. Each paragraph can stand alone, but it must also carry the pitch. Like we learned during the unfolding section in the book, use connecting words like *and, or,* and *but* to create the flow and help guide the story. Using these might help connect the sentences.

Repetition

When we speak, we tend to repeat ourselves over and over to make a point. When writing, we tend to avoid it, but repetition done right is a great way of getting the message across. You should be repeating your main goal three times throughout the pitch. You can have it appear first during your hook (when you first make your claim), repeat it further down (somewhere around where you have some good data proving that you are on the right path), and lastly, leave them with that message at the end. Repetition is a powerful tool to plant an idea subconsciously, but it should be subtle enough, concise enough, or it will sound too salesy. Worse still, it could sound boring and cause your audience to tune out.

It is important to avoid using repetition to fill the gaps if your pitch is too short. Repetition should be part of the story, not dropped into it or used as padding. Repeating too many messages might also confuse the audience. The friction point you want to hit is a balance between staying on message but using creative language to avoid boring or confusing the audience and using your catchphrases as anchor points.

Read your text and mark the sentences where repetition is apparent. Do you need all of them? What purpose does each repetition serve?

Decide which points to rewrite and which ones will serve you well if repeated. I once worked with an international fund. We wanted to repeat the fact that they had been successful in their previous funds. We made sure to drop a subtle mention in the hook, another one when discussing the number of investments they had made, and another mention when we got to the "ask" part of the story.

Repetition should be carefully chosen—like the right jewelry to complete and complement an outfit without drowning out the wearer or the dress.

Loose ends

Now you need to tie up loose ends. Has this presentation, the pitch, delivered on the promise it offered in the beginning? Have we answered every question we started with?

Often, startups, especially in complex solutions like manufacturing, tend to leave too many loose ends—that is, they deliver a pitch where one piece of information is missing the second proof point. One vital piece of information left out or left unclear might cause the whole story to collapse. A manufacturing startup failed to mention that the amazing solution they have is too complex for most factories, and thus too expensive. A water purification company explained their bot but not how the bot operates; a water electricity engine only shared the platform measures and produces without explaining the partnerships needed with factories. We understand some of it, but not all. Too many loose ends create a gap that might be solved if you have time for questions, but if you don't have time for questions, it might leave you with a confused audience.

Simplifying language

It was an online workshop; we had about ten days for the startups we were coaching to improve their stories before their investor demo day. As one founder finished his pitch, I was staring at my screen, occupied by about a dozen small squares

91

full of other confused people all waiting for me to say something. I thought about it for a few long seconds and then asked the presenter if I could share some tough love—the truth.

I'm not sure if he expected my reaction, but I apologized. I literally did not understand the product, the concept, or the solution. Between you and me, I could barely understand the English. His explanation was so technical it completely went over my head.

When writing your story, I recommend having three stories in one. Like a layer cake. Each story can be customized to the level of understanding your audience has, and you can present the correct layer to them. The first layer is the full, complete story as you will tell it in most meetings. It should be general enough for most people to understand. The second level will be a little more of a deep dive, as if you are presenting to investors or people in your company. Finally, the last version is for people in the know, like yourself—those from your industry, those who get it.

Define and prepare your presenting level. We know that language is the words we choose to use. Here, I want you to think a little more deeply about it. Think about the technical level we use to describe our project when presenting to a specific audience. In many cases, the pitch has only one version, with zero ability to adapt to different audiences. The best pitch is the one that can be adapted to suit the knowledge and technical ability of the audience, and it will allow you to stand out from the crowd.

Dumb it down

Back to that presenter I shared my feelings with. Trust me when I say I was lost. "I'm not dumb," I told him, "but I'm not well-versed in your industry. You had likely been working on this idea for a long time before you pitched it. You are a genius, and I will never know what you know about your business, but for me to help you, I need to understand what you are talking about in simple language."

A common misconception people make is thinking that if others don't understand them, they just don't get it. A better way to look at it is by asking yourself what could be done to prevent this from happening. If someone doesn't get it, it isn't about them as listeners. It's about us as communicators. We are the ones who haven't worked hard enough.

That's why it's important to create a story that fits everyone— the neighbor, the person at the bar, your mom, *anyone*. This will be your general pitch. The second one could be for people who understand the basics, the jargon, for investors interested in what you do. The last version is for technical people who get it, who understand everything you say, who work in your industry.

No one likes to feel dumb. In many cases, people will refrain from asking questions to avoid that feeling. This will be your loss. Do yourself a favor: make sure you talk at a level people understand. Dumb it down—not just for the audience but also to increase your chances of success. If they don't understand what you do and what's in it for them, they won't invest, believe, or take part. The cliché is true: keep it simple—stupidly simple.

The first minutes are your chance to leave an impression and make sure they want more of you, your idea, and your team. After that, you can drill down and go on another date; it's all open.

Accordion writing

Over the course of the book, we have worked on a trailer pitch version with approximately 500 words. It's essentially the three-minute demo-day concept.

I remember coaching a company for a competition held in Asia. The first round had three minutes per company with 50 companies pitching, but the finals offered a five-minute pitch. We worked in what I call an "accordion model," where we added more paragraphs to elaborate where needed. We ended up adding only one minute. It was more than enough to take out first place. More time means more information, so choose wisely where you can enhance what has been said; avoid just adding text for the sake of adding. Most probably, your pitch is trimmed, so an example, a product, or a client option could be helpful.

When you feel your story is good enough to share, it's time to get feedback. Do not wait until it is perfect. If you put your heart and soul into it, it will be harder to implement the feedback provided. I would suggest sharing the written version with several people but also reading it out loud to your team members or people you trust. You will be surprised how different people perceive the same piece of text. Reading for others will help you make sure the text sounds the way you intend it to be.

Share, learn, repeat

The editing process never ends. There is no perfect; there is just better. It works best when we keep iterating, by ourselves and with others. Share the story, written or spoken. Get people's reactions. Learn from it. Edit again. The first version might be rubbish. Don't worry, though. It is just the first try, but the tenth or the fiftieth version will be so far away from where you are now—so much better, sleeker. Constant improvement is needed. Tweaking is the name of the game. The true work, in many cases, starts when you finish writing. It starts when you edit.

Keep in mind that eventually you have to draw a line under it. You have to stop editing and deliver your pitch. Maybe deadlines decide the endpoint. Or maybe you reach the part of the bell-curve where every new iteration only reaps differences rather than improvements. Then you know you're there.

Exercise

Start with the plot points and paragraphs you have from the previous chapter. Start filling in the blanks and reviewing what you've written with an emphasis on using the tools discussed in this chapter. Ask yourself: Does each paragraph efficiently convey an important message? Are my transitions between sentences and paragraphs smooth and logical? Can I use repetition to emphasize an important point? Have I tied up all loose ends? Is the language simple enough?

Chapter 9
Writing and Editing

Your hook

Use the sentence to create a paragraph under it

1

2

3

Keep doing this for each of the plot lines you created

10

BALANCE AND KPIS

Percentage

"Is it good? What do you think?" he asks as I quietly read on the other side of the online call. My cursor starts selecting paragraphs and adding the word count numbers next to each one. About 40% of the pitch is dedicated to two subjects: the market potential and the competition. "What is the key message here?" I ask, to which he replies, "I want them to understand we can take on the market, and if we can just get a small percentage, it's huge money."

"That is a rational thing they will understand. They are smart. They wouldn't take this meeting if they weren't interested in making money, but what is the one key message? What will they understand from this paragraph, and what feeling should it provoke?" I asked.

We continued to discuss his pitch for some time. Eventually, it reached a point where he couldn't hide his frustration: "But how can I know if my story is balanced? If it works?"

It got me thinking that he might be on to something. *How can you measure your trailer pitch?*

Working on what could serve as KPIs, the key performance indicators to a story, it soon became clear. We can measure three things: the length of the text, the key message it conveys, and the feelings expressed to the audience. Moving back and forth between these three creates more than just a balanced paragraph. It brings complete balance to the whole story, from top to bottom, and a balanced story works.

Let's look at 500-word trailer pitch as an example.

Step 1: Divide up the pitch. In a three-minute pitch, we can have eight to ten paragraphs, and the hook is the most important, equating to about 15% or roughly the first 30 seconds. The summary will be about 10%, which leaves 75% to share between everything else.

Step 2: Look at the body of the pitch, the paragraphs. A short paragraph will have about 30–40 words, and a longer one around 55 words. Once you have measured these—and before you panic and start cutting things out—let's check if the paragraph even says what you want it to say and how it serves the need.

Step 3: Define your key messages. What is the one key message you want them to take from each paragraph? Read each one and ensure you can extract the key message—just one *clear* message. What is written and what is understood are not always the same thing. If you explain the market size, we hear potential. When you present your team, the thought in everyone's mind is whether they can be trusted.

So, refine your key message in each paragraph or rewrite the text. Add each key message on the right of every paragraph. Ensure the paragraphs make sense, that they flow, and make sure that they do not repeat the same key message twice. Key messages ensure you keep your text clean from irrelevant data and information. This will be done in the editing stage, over and over, until it's crisp and clear. It will also guarantee your audience understands what you are trying to convey.

Step 4: Improve your key messages. A great way of improving the key message is reading the paragraph once it's been taken out of context. Just read it by itself. Now try and extract the key message. It should be a single line explaining not what you have just read but what you should understand from what you have read.

Step 5: Clean it up. Now re-read the original paragraph and extract the data points—the things you are telling the audience. You might be surprised at how many things you've tried to cram in there. Make a list of them and ask yourself: Does this support my key message? Or can I remove it?

Step 6: Attach feelings and emotions. Next to the key message, we will add the feelings for each paragraph. Adding three feelings gives your paragraph emotional layers, from descriptive to very deep. One word describing a feeling might not be enough, so using the circle of feelings can help you. We aim to take the audience on a journey with us—to make them feel excitement, trust, and intrigue, to make them wonder, hope, and believe it can be done.

For many, attaching feelings to a key message and finding the feelings to express intentions is one of the hardest things. Stories are meant to teach us and make us feel. It can be as simple as adding the list of feelings you want people to feel in each paragraph and ensuring those emotions are flowing correctly throughout your story.

There is more than one way to make a story stick, so we use feelings to control how our audience will perceive the messages. This combination of message and feeling, of rational and emotional, solidifies your story in their brains, encouraging them to agree with what they are hearing. This combination is your way of influencing them to think and feel a certain way about you and your pitch. An engaging story will make them agree and nod their heads. When the story and feelings are consistent, growing from one paragraph to the next, it will amplify your story; they will be rooting for you, wanting to join your cause, thinking about what success might look like if they join you.

PEOPLE ARE SMART, intuitive creatures. The audience will sense your unintentional feelings, such as being nervous or making a wisecrack to ease your tension, and they can relate because it is likely they once had to present in a situation where they felt the same as you. They are also able to feel your conviction and dedication in solving the problem because they also want to feel what you are feeling—or, even better, they know how it feels to stumble on the solution for a problem. When the emotions are not written down, you might accidentally send the wrong message, leaving the other side to fill the gap from their own experience.

Examples of feelings to attach to different paragraphs

When talking about our product, we tend to go deep into technical information to satisfy the audience, who is eager to understand if this could work and, if so, whether they will be part of changing the world for the better. The key message should be "It works," and the attached feelings might be hope, excitement, and interest in learning how it works.

The TAM (total addressable market)

Every company can claim the total addressable market is in the billions of dollars or potential clients. The size of the market is also not the key message but, rather, the potential for success. This might be well connected in many cases to the competition section, showing there is still space in the market for new players like yourself. It creates reassurance, lower risk, and willingness to try.

The team

When presenting the team members, we aspire to show we have chosen the right people capable of getting the job done. The key message could be, "We are the right people to go to war with, even if things might change or if the idea needs to pivot." The feelings associated with this are trust, respect, and collaboration.

The roadmap

Explaining our roadmap shows we are realistic in our plans; we have done the research and have clear goals of where we are going next. The feelings associated with this could be grounded, responsible, and organized.

Keep in mind ...

When a miscorrelation occurs—when what we say does not resonate with the other side or something feels wrong—the other side will either raise concerns or avoid the risk by bailing from your story, preferring to go with someone else's pitch. That's why we want to make sure that, whether in words or emotions, there are no disconnects or misattributions.

While the story is the spine, our KPIs are built on top, helping us keep track not only of what we are saying but also of how we plan on delivering that story. You might be nervous. You might get confused. Using the key messages and feelings to your advantage will help you pass what you meant on, even if what you said came out different than expected.

Exercise

Try reading each paragraph out loud to make sure each makes sense on its own. We always have at least two students working in my agency, Streetwise, to gain some experience. One of the best practices we recommend for them is to read their emails out loud. This offers insight into what they wrote versus what the reader might understand. Try it—it's a great exercise.

Chapter 10
Complete your KPIs

#	Text	%	Key Message	Feelings

11

NOW THAT YOU'RE NOT DEPENDENT ON SLIDES, LET'S MAKE SOME SLIDES

I know what you're thinking: *What the f*ck?*

I was in Lisbon, Portugal. It was the Web Summit conference, one of the biggest tech events in the world, and I'd been asked to host and present the startups in a deep tech competition. Everything was going well until the second contestant got on stage and found that the slides on the screens belonged not to them but to the third group. The founder stopped, at a loss. I got on stage to explain the technical error. And my t-shirt said—you guessed it—*F*ck the Slides* in big letters.

The audience laughed, and as we were waiting, I offered for the founder to keep going without slides for extra points from our four judges. His first reaction was *I can't do it.* Two long minutes passed, and just as he decided to try without the slides, his slides were found, and he presented.

Unfortunately, his slides were all wrong. Instead of helping, they were hurting him. I know we are expected to have slides in our pitches. Even you expect it from yourself. That's fine. We use slides when presenting in front of investors, at work, and as students. People expect you to have slides. It's just the way it is, and it has been for several decades now. Some investors might even see not having slides as a form of disrespect, that you came unprepared.

As I have previously mentioned in this book, F*ck the Slides is not about avoiding slides at all but rather switching the order of importance: write the story and design the slides later, instead of wrapping the spoken pitch around the slides and hoping it sticks. We learned that the spine is our written story, and that everything else is added on top of that. I would argue that we are misusing the slides instead of making them work for us. It is time we redefine and distill the role of slides and understand how to incorporate them into the story.

You are doing it the wrong way.

My claim is that most slides are hurting the story instead of elevating it. A visual element should make us look better, helping us get the message across, but when it comes to slides, we tend to overcrowd them. We read them out loud. We show them at the wrong time. We let the slides control our pace. We are making our audience work hard or making them wait. Either way, it's not good. We are doing it all wrong. And where we lose the game, it's biology—our visual and hearing senses. Yep, it's all about the way our mind is wired. Luckily, this common mistake is the easiest thing to solve.

You see, no matter how hard we try, our eyes will gravitate toward the visual, and our attention will divert from the speaker. As much as we might try and fight it, our eyes tend to wander to the slide, trying to make sense, figuring it all out. If your slide has twenty words and an image or two, the audience requires a few good seconds to figure it all out.

Sadly, we can't process information and listen at the same time. Eyesight will almost always win in a competition against our ability to listen to the speaker.

It's like being at home, watching your favorite show with your spouse. You are bingeing through the episodes, just the two of you, until you need to go to the toilet. But you really don't want to stop the episode, so you decide to go quickly, asking them to keep watching. In two minutes, you're back under the blanket again. You both smile, but now you've missed a part. You try to work it out—until you crack and have to ask what you just missed. They get mad. Familiar?

You just did that to your audience with your slides. In a short, three-minute pitch, you lost them. You distracted them. They were reading, not listening to your story. Now they are trying to play catch up, while others are going to just give up and wait until you finish. You have ended up with a polite audience that couldn't keep up.

If they are reading while you speak, they are not listening. If you are reading from the slide, they are waiting for you to finish, and no one likes waiting. You can read four or five times faster than you can speak. They are now ahead of you, waiting for you to finish. It's subconscious: no one likes to wait.

Another common mistake with slides is knowing whether to present them before, during, or after we speak about the matter. In many cases, we use the slides as a path to navigate the pitch—but remember, the slides are meant for the audience, not for you. Figure out when would be the right time to expose the slide. When will it serve you best in strengthening the story? Slides should be reinforcing your message instead of just giving you something to click through for appearance's sake.

Types of slides

While working on your trailer pitch, you will have to decide on several types of slides showcasing the problem, solution, and market potential, among other things. You will also need to decide on the content style—everything from text to images, pie charts, tables, and more. But I would like to discuss what purpose the visual on each slide will serve in helping you get your message across. We want to ensure our audience sees, feels, and understands your key message. I therefore like to divide the slides into two types.

The scenery slide

The first slide type is the "scenery" slide, a direct extension of what you are saying. The scenery is just there to support what you are saying, to strengthen your key message in a visual way, helping your audience agree with you. Whether it is just an image, graphs, or information, it will be directly connected to what you are verbally presenting. Some examples might include your roadmap slide or how much you are looking to raise. You will explain these while speaking. An image when you show your product could also serve as your scenery, helping the audience understand, making sure the message sticks.

The supporting-role slide

When slides have more information than you have presented so far, this is referred to as the "supporting role," helping you introduce things that might be of importance but that you will not talk about. When presenting your features slide, you will introduce many new pieces of information but only go through the relevant ones. The same goes when showcasing the competition.

A side note here: try and avoid showing your newly established company as better than the old, big tech giants. It creates a lack of trust, making you seem out of focus.

Let's talk design

Working with designers this way, sharing your story and a complete brief, is very useful, as the audience can finally see the complete picture. I have seen people present incredible slides, well-connected to the pitch—and yet, some investors did not like what they saw. Designing the slides is a very subjective matter.

One of the biggest challenges designers often face is understanding what is required of them. It's in understanding how the slides support the pitch and strengthening the connection between the spoken word and the visual. Done properly, it will make the audience feel the slides are exactly how they should be: part of the story, not a distraction. Stripping away needless data and design elements will help them create a relevant trailer pitch deck with as few distractions as possible. If it doesn't move you forward, drop it. If it doesn't serve a purpose, take it out. Anything put into a trailer pitch slide equates to eyeballs focusing more on the visual and that much less on you and your message. Trust that their brain will complete the image. They heard you. They understand.

So much has been said about the correct way to design slides. Having one clear message is crucial, as is limiting the information and controlling what the eye sees and in which order. We could discuss font style and size, but I will leave this part to your designers. Focus on the one key thing the slides need to show, whether it is one sentence to support your message, a large number, or just one image to help the imagination run in the right direction.

No "thank you"

Please, please, PLEASE do not have your last slide read "Thank you." Trust me, nobody cares. You will say thank you when you finish, but the last slide just might be the most high-value real estate you could have during your trailer pitch. The last slide is your chance to summarize, to leave them with one last final thought as you are closing your pitch, so saying thank you is a waste. During certain presentations, this slide might stay on longer than any other. There might be questions. The next presenter might be delayed. There are many things that could cause your last slide to stay up in full view, even after you've left the stage.

True, in many cases, it will disappear just when you finish speaking, but in others, it will last for a minute longer, enough time for the audience to see it. This is your chance to repeat your message. Leave that rhetorical question or the thought-provoking idea you wanted them to remember you for.

Exercise

It is time we build your confidence, connect the spoken word with design. Focus on your pitch and telling your story without any slides. The aim of this exercise is to learn how to rely less on visual aids and feel more comfortable practicing your presentation. Next, consider what types of slides can support your message in each part of your story, whether a scenery or supporting slide. Add a column next to each paragraph with your slide choice and another column for the information you would like to provide in each slide.

Remember: the audience is there primarily to listen to you, not read what's behind you.

Chapter 11
Adding slides

#	Text	Type of slide	Visual on slide

12

EVERYTHING ELSE— BEFORE, DURING, AND AFTER THE MEETING

She agreed to a five-minute meeting outside the main hall. That is all the time she could spare—and well, it was enough for her to come off as polite with committing to anything. It was so informal; she had a seat, and I leaned on the reception table. She expected a quick pitch explaining why I needed money, but she received a glimpse into the future and how she would feel as a winner when we achieved our goal together. The meeting was short. She agreed to talk more—no commitments. The moment the meeting was up, the deck reached her inbox, showing I meant business and I could back up my words. With a few more calls, adapting the content for each call, I managed to secure $350,000 of funding to build a new global marketing agency.

We have gone over the trailer pitch as the opener; if done correctly, it should help you pass to the next step. In this chapter, we will cover the other things you should prepare for before, during, and after the meeting.

In today's market, interactions can vary from a casual talk to a long meeting. We present or compete against other presenters for the same attention, each with their own needs and expectations, and we should also be ready to adapt. Most founders use the same deck for everything, but as we have learned by now, the trailer pitch slides require less text—so what happens after the trailer pitch, when they ask you for more information before, during, or after the meeting?

The toilet deck

What started as a joke became the toilet deck, or the TD for short. The name "toilet deck" came to life with the realization that many people go over decks in their free time while sitting on the toilet, and the need to emphasize that you will not sit next to them while they do so.

A common mistake is using the same slide for presenting as you do for sending out. Don't do this.

In the first scenario, when we are pitching, WE are the presentation, remember? In your pitch slide deck, there should be very little text, if any. It should be virtually impossible for someone to look at your trailer pitch slides and understand anything without your verbal pitch.

By contrast, the slides for your TD need to hold on their own. These slides need to tell a visual story with just enough text to get your idea and potential through without imposing too much reading. The slide is not a novel.

Ask yourself: what is the purpose of the TD? It's not to get the check, it's to get the next meeting. A great way to do this would be to use your trailer pitch story and adapt it into a visual story.

I once received a 32-slide deck from someone I'd never met. He was referred by a colleague inquiring about my team's marketing services. Thirty-two slides felt so long, with technical explainers and deep dives into the budgets. It felt like a presentation they probably sent out to secure venture capital and kept using when the feedback was good. Many years ago, we used to send a twelve-page PDF to a potential client. It included every service we could offer with a full explainer. The good thing was the first and last pages: *why we are good at what we do* was the first and *what will happen to your marketing if you choose to work with us* was the last. I doubt if anyone ever read the 10 pages in the middle. But it looked amazing, and it got us meetings.

TD 1 and TD 2

To really go to the next level, prepare two TD's: one for before the meeting and one for after. The first is what I've just described, a visual story of your trailer pitch. The second, after they have met you, and you have presented the Babylon deck described below, is an extension of the trailer pitch with expanded details. The "after" TD is more technical, and less story based. They get the story, the emotion—now this second TD's goal is to expand and convince the rational mind that the emotional one is correct, and this is a good investment to make.

Tip: When you send the "after" TD, mention in the title that this is a post-meeting deck.

During the meeting—Babylon deck

You sent them the TD, you got the meeting and you have given them your trailer pitch. They like it. Now it is time to jump into the discussion—the clarifying questions. During this stage, people want to learn more about you and your work. They will assess your knowledge and experience and your ability to deliver on your pitch promise.

This stage is just as much about you as it is about the data you are about to share. This is your chance to create trust, show humility, listen, and leave a mark—the type that will open doors for the next stage, winning them over.

This is where the Babylon deck comes in. I chose to name it Babylon because in ancient times, it was the capital of the empire, said to have been the largest city at one point. It is considered the birthplace of science and knowledge. It is said that all the answers in ancient times were there. The Babylon deck will serve as an appendix for everything.

Anything that might be of interest during the meeting but didn't make the cut into the trailer pitch could go here, into the Babylon deck. This is the deck that has an answer to everything we might be asked. Coming prepared with answers by pre-answering them shows you put thought into it and that you know what you are talking about. This creates that trust and professionalism you would like to show your audience.

The Babylon deck can have as many slides as needed, answering questions that arise during the conversation. One of my clients had 67 slides by the time they raised all the questions they felt needed to be answered. They collected questions from meeting to meeting, designing slides for the relevant ones and adding them.

During each session, they only shared the relevant ones, but they came prepared in case the subjects popped up. The slides could serve a more data-driven approach, including more information, graphs, and screenshots—even videos. You might have time and they might want you want to go deeper. While in meetings, take notes of questions that might be relevant for future meetings and make sure you add them to your Babylon deck.

Revisiting TD 2

After the meeting, you will have a great idea of what matters to the investor based on their questions and feedback in the meeting. Customize TD 2 with slides from the Babylon deck that the investor thought were relevant before you send it over.

The one-pager

Although I believe we can safely say the one-pager concept is dead, I felt it would be important to address it. Today, most send a deck, a short description—but rarely do they include the full old-school one-pager.

I remember days when we tried sending two pages as a one-pager and some investors gave us crap about it, but we just couldn't make everything fit on one page. I can recount long nights working on those for my clients, always feeling it wasn't clear enough. We would try to squeeze everything in: a tagline, the team pictures, a graph, maybe a pie chart of the market size or competition. Trying to get it all in meant size-nine fonts. Luckily, the industry grew out of it. Technology helped the one-pager morph from the old printed A4 page. We stopped printing physical pages. Decks became the norm, then longer PDFs. Some build one-page websites or use apps such as Notion Templates.

Sadly, many founders still make the same mistakes, trying to squeeze in too much text, too much information, an old way of doing things into a new medium.

In my opinion, the old one-pager is obsolete, but we can learn from it. It will never return. Approach everything as if you do not have enough real estate for everything. Extracting the essence from each section of your pitch in a line or two is a great exercise, and doing it will always help you. It's just like we learned in the "what" and "how" sections. It will apply to your business model, team members, and product. Keep it concise, short, and simple.

A blurb about you

"Send me a blurb about you."

"Shoot me a blurb with some info when you get the chance."

Blurb. I love this word. Not necessarily very common around the world, but useful when asked to send a short explainer describing yourself and your work.

The word *blurb* originated over a hundred years ago, coined by American humorist Gelett Burgess. He introduced the blurb—a short description for any piece of content to accompany the creative work, making people want it. It was introduced first in the book industry and later used in films and other industries.

The blurb is a combination of promotion and selling, spiced with creativity, highlighting what's in it for the reader. It has since become synonymous with asking for a short explainer—what you and your company are all about.

In today's tech industry, we must introduce ourselves countless times. Some people might ask for the verbal elevator pitch, while others want a quick written blurb. The elevator pitch has changed, morphed into so many different things, and still, people dread it even though they might be asked to tell it very often. Written or verbal, on a podcast or during a short elevator ride, a good blurb will go a long way. My suggestion is to prepare another blurb version so it will be able to serve you on almost every occasion.

The blurb how-to

The blurb will be divided into four parts:

1. the "what" you do one-liner,
2. a "how" paragraph,
3. the story hook, and
4. another paragraph about you.

What you do is your ear-catcher, something that will stick in their mind and is easy to remember.

The "how" is the elaboration. As we have learned before, it should be about 60–70 words long.

The hook you previously designed can be an excellent starter, explaining everything—especially in a casual conversation—thus creating interest without sending you off track, talking too much, or adding unnecessary info. You can try pitching the hook first, ending with the "what" one-liner.

Finally, you should include a very short paragraph about yourself. It should be in the context of your company in a way that sheds enough light to confirm that you are professional and experienced and that you know what you are talking about. Put this last unless specifically asked to talk about yourself. The business is the important thing.

When it's done, your blurb should equate to two short paragraphs in writing. The what, the how, and the hook in the first, and the paragraph about yourself as the second.

Depending on your speaking speed, this would be about one minute, to say about 140 words—enough time to cover everything in a short elevator ride or a short email.

Each of these four could stand by themselves or in a different order, so try different orders and see what works best for you.

Plan the session

Whether you've got three minutes in a demo day, ten minutes to pitch, a fifteen-minute online call, or an hour-long meeting, planning is crucial. Just like we write and practice the trailer pitch, evaluating and planning the meeting steps will help you win more often. Define your meeting goals and plan the answers for the most-asked questions to ensure you don't just waste time or say something that you didn't plan on sharing. And true, we can only plan for what we know, but you will learn that it will help you get more out of every session.

It's true, we can only plan for what we know and what we expect, but you will learn that preparation will help you get more out of every session.

What about everything else, the unknown?

Be agile—adapt and know you did your best. You showed up, you came prepared, and that is more than 99% of people ever do.

Exercise

Let's focus on creating your blurb. Have a try! See what you can create.

Chapter 12
The blurb

The "what" you do one-liner

a "how" paragraph

Your hook

About you

13

THE SHOW

During my sessions, I sometimes share this, and people still do not believe me. Many years ago, I suffered from stage fright. Sure, I was funny around friends, I could tell a story in front of strangers—but standing on stage or giving a big talk was a problem.

My heartbeat would soar; I would start to sweat, and the first few minutes would always be so stressful. Sometimes I would forget what I wanted to say. But when I decided it was a skill to master, I worked hard and improved, and when I felt it was time, I went back to my college, this time to be a teacher. Just to be clear, *there is no "perfect,"* and even while I work as hard as I can, I have had some bad talks. The good thing is, those bad talks, like scars on my back, I'll remember for years to come. They are the lessons, the reminders that we can always do better, so long as we learn the lessons.

But how can we ensure our story comes out the way we planned? What turns it into a successful show?

Practice

It is time we train our body to play the part. We have it all written down. Our most important 7%, the verbal communication part, is ready. We have defined everything we want to pass on to our audience. Now it is time to help our body pass on those other non-verbal pieces of communication. Confidence will come across well, even if you forget a line or mention the wrong data point. The more we practice, the better we will feel, the better our editing will become—but, more importantly, the more our body will remember how to behave.

Comfort and confidence happen when we practice. We go from being nervous about what we say to embracing how we want to say it. High tone, open arms, or low voice, head down, same sentence—it amounts to a completely different impact. Everything we have done so far helps us define how it should be performed. Following the next steps will transform your skill from writing to speaking, to being a master storyteller.

Start by reading your text out loud a few times. Timing yourself could be helpful to make sure you are close or around the time planned. Speaking the text over and over is all about getting the intonation just right. Although it is rarely part of the preparation, intonation plays a crucial role in effective communication during a presentation. It refers to the rise and fall of pitch in our voice as we speak, and it can convey emotions, attitudes, and emphasis. Utilizing proper intonation can significantly enhance the impact of your presentation and engage your audience in a meaningful way. Paragraph by paragraph, the key message and feelings you added to the trailer pitch will serve you as notes do a musician, each one reflecting how to use your voice.

For example, a monotone voice can be dull and uninspiring, while varied intonation can express enthusiasm, excitement, or urgency. By using the list, you will know how happy or sad one might feel, for example, when talking about the dire situation of the environment or the solution at hand. In addition, intonation can emphasize key points and ideas. By placing stress on important words or phrases through changes in pitch, you can highlight their significance and make them stand out in the minds of your audience. This can help reinforce your main message and ensure that your key points are memorable.

With feeling

Read your paragraphs with the intent to convey the feelings you have written down. You know how these feelings look and sound—you have been using them your whole life. Remember, you smile, they smile; the transaction of emotions occurs. Speed, pace, pause, and rhythm are significant elements while you're presenting. A slow, repetitive speed is mind-numbing to the audience, but if you speak too fast, you will lose them. When deciding on speed, try different variations.

Breathing while reading is imperative. Having clear and well-structured sentences creates that pace; it allows you to breathe and sound calm, confident. Often, we tend to start too fast, as if we are throwing our speech onto the crowd, trying to get it over and done with. Where speed is needed, go for it, but otherwise, make sure your pace is regulated throughout the presentation. Find your normal speaking pace, the speed where you feel comfortable most of the time, and go out of that when creating an emphasis, a bold statement. Inserting a pause to create drama is a useful tool, but you can only use it so much, and the same goes for asking the audience questions. Leaving them with food for thought could be done with a question in the last part of the pitch, giving them something to think about after the presentation has ended.

Once these are in place and well-rehearsed, they will also reflect your confidence and credibility as a speaker. A well-modulated voice with appropriate intonation can make you sound confident, knowledgeable, and authoritative, enhancing your overall presentation delivery and impression on your audience.

English is the common presentation language, and as someone whose first language ISN'T English, this is more than just a side note. Bear in mind that your accent is a part of the show. It says something about you too, whether you realize it or not.

You have different experiences, different perspectives, to native English speakers. Different can be worldly; it can make investors realize they don't know everything about what is happening in every part of the world. You may see something they don't, so lean into that.

As far as the actual presentation goes, mispronouncing an English word can be jarring for an English speaker and take them out of your story. Review the words you struggle with in terms of accent. If a word is hard to pronounce, replace it.

I have worked with people with heavy accents, and even my accent is hard to understand at times. What I've realized is I need to emphasize certain words more than I would while casually speaking. We will not change our accent, but there is no reason to make it hard on ourselves or the audience. I once worked with an amazing guy who had a heavy Russian accent I could barely understand. When we finished working on his story, he spent time polishing his accent. He raised money soon after.

Video

For many people, seeing themselves on video is not a comfortable thing, even in today's digital video frenzy. If that is the case for you, this can the fastest and most valuable way you can improve your odds of success. For years I wouldn't even have my picture taken, and to this day, recording myself on video feels uncomfortable, but I understand the benefits of being good on video.

Take it one step at a time. For the first rounds, you might use an audio recording, but for the non-verbal communication part of your pitch, video is what's needed. You've spent time developing a really great pitch, so just start by reading it online into a program like Loom or Zoom, or some other digital platform.

It will become very apparent—from pace to losing the key message with the wrong intonation—what you need to fix. Make a list of everything you need to fix and go again. Review it, make a new list, then go again. You will notice the same mistakes repeating themselves. It is normal.

As you get used to the camera, you will begin to feel your tension disappear; your pace will settle down, and you will feel as if you have done this a million times before. Once you are comfortable, you can start to work on your list, fixing one thing at a time.

I often ask for permission to record my calls to review and improve later. I will even ask to only record my pitch, if possible, so people can speak freely before and after. For some, that shows another part of being serious about improving. When reviewing a pitch recording, don't be too harsh on yourself. If you aim to improve three small things, after the next ten meetings, you will be amazed at how much your presentation has improved.

Writing a story and telling a story are two different skills. These two skills go hand in hand, and not having one or the other could be detrimental to your success. As you keep rehearsing over and over, you will feel you have it all figured out. The story is there. But I would argue that it is at about 80%. The closest analogy here would be the comic's mindset. You see, stand-up comics are relentless in their work. They are willing to do it again and again until it's perfect. They will start in the smallest places, get the feedback, fall flat on their faces, then get up and try again. For them, failing is just another step in their journey of crafting their best jokes, making every small nuance work. The comedian mindset is an insatiable desire to get the perfect punch every time.

Online pitching

I love online pitching. I know most of you will disagree with me, but, like them or hate them, online meetings are here to stay. As my clients are global, I pitch online quite often, whether to clients or when working with founders about to pitch online themselves—I love it. Turning these short online pitching calls can be to your advantage.

Follow these tips. They are easy to follow, and although setting them up might be annoying, you will be surprised at how helpful they are. Not following these tips means you are leaving the biggest part of your communication—your body language—out of the game. Now, I'm sure you will want to use every advantage you can to win the pitch.

Stand up

Stand up in every pitching call to generate the power dynamics: this creates a physical and psychological hierarchy, where the speaker is elevated above the audience. This difference in physical positioning can create a perception of power or authority, with the speaker being seen as "above" the audience, both literally and metaphorically. This can lead to a psychological imbalance, where the speaker is perceived as having more power or knowledge, and the audience may be more inclined to listen and comply.

Wide shot

The second step is having a medium-wide shot—for three reasons. It will take the focus away from your facial gestures. During a normal pitch, these gestures will only account for some of the things the audience looks at. Online calls turn these into the main thing, not always serving the best purpose. A face closeup can be monotonous, as people see the same image for a long period of time. Lastly, but perhaps most importantly, a medium shot brings you back to life, moving, adding hand gestures to your verbal pitch. This brings back the body language aspect—the most important piece in communication, remember?

Another great effect online speaking has is the ability to move back and forth, adding another dimension to the call. Not only are you not static—your size varies during your movements—but as you move closer to the camera, something happens that cannot be duplicated in a real pitch: you can literally speak to everyone. When zooming into the camera, everyone on the other side of the call will feel as if they are the only person there. This powerful element can be used as part of non-verbal communication to emphasize something of importance.

Exercise

Choose one paragraph and read it out loud.

Then, read the same paragraph as if you are thrilled to read it.

Now, try it as if you are sad about the content.

Use the key message, the feelings you have next to the paragraph, and read what you have written over and over, at least five times. Try to remember the paragraph by heart.

The more you read it, the more it feels natural.

Chapter 13
The show

Key message   Feelings

After each read, take notes to keep improving

1

2

3

4

5

14

LIFE HACKS

A startup might need a hundred meetings before finding an investment. A service provider might need ten to fifteen leads to close one. It is not a black or white world. We make mistakes, we learn, we keep going. My students often remind me that I do not understand how hard it is for them, even though I went through it to some degree. The same goes for salespeople believing it's the hardest time to find clients because the market is down. You are not the first to face and overcome these challenges. Remember that. We go through so many hardships on our journey, and we forget that many have walked down the same path we are about to take. When going into meetings, come prepared, and know that the outcome might not be in your favor, but if you have given it your all, there is always another way, another chance, another meeting ...

Over the years, I have compiled many mistakes I have made, saw others make, or believe you might need to avoid when you go into future meetings to present. These are divided in an easy way to help you improve over time, but one thing, to summarize them all—my one ask of you—is to adopt a learner's mindset. When we take a different approach, when we choose to look at everything from a learning perspective with respect to those around us, we realize that not everything is failure. Rather, it is another lesson on our journey. *Fail, fail fast, learn, embrace, fix, and go at it again.* This chapter is a compilation of experience shares—things you should be sure to add to your list, things to take note of, and some behaviors to avoid.

Don't fall in love

The world is filled with those amazing success stories, the founders who never gave up, even when everyone else told them they would fail. But the world has more untold stories of those who wouldn't let go when it was time.

Years ago, I met a young founder. Smart, dedicated, he was on a mission to disrupt an industry. I thought his business model was not viable but decided to introduce him to some more experienced folks from that industry. They all agreed that the idea was good but not viable; he couldn't raise capital. But, no matter what everyone said, he wouldn't listen—he had fallen in love with his own idea. He remained stubborn. He lost his money; the business never made it, and he wasted more than three years of his life. Be ready to have an honest conversation with yourself. Define your success metrics, time, money, clients, wins—any type that suits your needs—and after that, know when it is time to stop. If you believe you, personally, have done enough but the idea is not valid, the business can't make it, consider your next moves carefully, but don't fall in love with your idea.

People are everything

You would be surprised how quick we are to judge the people in front of us, even though we never really know them. The people you meet on this journey—who they really are or who they might become, what they could become for you or vice versa. People are people; each one can help. Some might be billionaires in flip flops, other times, students who will go on to build big things. The power of networking, helping, and supporting will play a huge role, no matter where you go. Respect people regardless of their job title; remind yourself that there is something to learn from everyone. That is a major reason why I love teaching young students—they never cease to amaze me. Each semester, I learn and improve just by spending time with them. During tough times, many people helped me build my company; many of them remembered that I had helped them when I could. Don't be an ass. Be kind.

Taking advice

Many believe the best thing is to talk to as many people as possible—those doing the same thing, on the same path, mentors. I get it: they just did it.

Everyone has an opinion, and they are eager to share their advice, which is great, but it's exactly that: just some advice. Over the years, I have noticed a problem, mainly in accelerators and hubs. Each week, the founders meet inspiring and successful people to hear their thoughts and get advice. The problem starts with these two key things: advice and inspiration. After every session, these founders go out of their way to adapt everything according to what they've heard. These frequent changes take the focus from the story and turn the pitch to jelly. Advice is just that, *subjective*, and it's on you to decide what fits your needs. Another thing to remember is to be mindful when asking for people to share their experience. They only know what you have told them—your one-sided story, not the whole story—so asking for their advice is a bit of a tricky ask. Listen, write, organize, and move forward in a structured way. Understand what fits you, what is advice, and what is a learning you could implement.

Just answer the question

The questions and answers (Q&A) section is an excellent opportunity to share a little bit more about yourself and your work. Q&A sessions in competitions differ from meetings in that they are often limited to five to ten minutes. This is your opportunity to shine, yet most people respond with long responses to short questions, focusing on what the judges might want to hear regardless of the question.

Respond effectively and to the point, giving them the opportunity to ask additional questions. During meetings, it may appear that there is an infinite amount of time to share information; nevertheless, trying to oversell will result in the opposite reaction. Give them the correct response, stick to the methodology, and answer the question—don't give them the *I'll say anything and hope something sticks* type of answer.

Don't argue

Often, tech founders go into a meeting hoping to get raving reviews, but when that turns into questions and doubts, they tend to argue, defending their idea instead of understanding the investor's point of view. You put in the work, come prepared, but the reaction is not exactly what you expected—it happens. Leave a good impression. Ask questions, take the input, and keep going. Arguing during a meeting never ends well. Even a small argument with a potential client could kill the meeting, as both sides might defend an idea instead of finding the positive. Be open to feedback and even criticism—maybe this is not a solution for everyone. We know, it's your baby and some of the things being said are not easy to hear, but this pushback creates antagonism. Listen, understand, absorb.

Clarify when needed; never argue. This is your chance to get as much as you can out of this conversation. In many cases, your behavior in this session will reflect heavily on what people in the room think about you. Ask for more and shut up. This is one of the ways you can earn trust.

"I don't know" is an answer

Sometimes, we do not have all the answers, and that is alright, as long as we are honest and communicate it during the session. It is far better to explain that you do not know, informing them that you will check and get back to them with an answer. Then actually do it.

Honesty creates trust. In the case of losing it, choking, or just going blank, tell them. You'll be surprised how many people in the room have felt what you are going through. Make them feel—they will be there for you.

Stand behind what you say; don't lie. It's that simple. I have worked with companies that tried to sugarcoat numbers. There are many ways to present data, but once you start going into the grey area, and you are not sure if you feel comfortable with it, stop and think again. A small lie might amplify and become a nightmare. And we are lying to our partners, investors, clients—these are the people who trust us. And we lie once, a small lie, we lie twice, and we lose track of the small lies. If you feel you are lying to yourself, you are certainly lying to someone else. Credibility is your currency. Go in in good faith, believing honesty will help you solve the issues—and if not, maybe it's for the better.

Follow up

I can't stress enough how important the follow-up process is in everything we do. Part of your meeting, of your pitch, should include this step—when, who, and what type of follow up you would like to have. It could be to get the deal going, ask for feedback, or just thank them for their time. This is also a chance to start a relationship, offering help and following up at a later date with an update or just asking after their wellbeing, offering each person the opportunity to reach out again.

Even bad meetings can turn good with a positive follow-up if you indicate that they are the important person by asking for their input. Even a complete polite-as-it-might-be *NO* is a growth opportunity. Thank them and ask for honest feedback. A good idea would be to have a list with a few topics you already know you would like to improve on. It could be your pitch, product, pricing—anything that comes to mind. This way, if they agree, you can make sure you cover everything you need and not just what comes to mind in the moment. When asking for feedback, it is imperative you do not defend your idea; this is an intelligence-gathering mission. It still surprises me how much information people are willing to divulge.

Ask for the chance to get back to them again with updated information or the next time you pitch. It will surprise you how many people would be happy to help you.

Learn from every session

The presentation is over. People are clapping. You smile, pick up your stuff, and let the next person come up to take their turn. When asked, "How was it?" you might reply, "Yeah, I feel good. It went well," taking a guess, only to later learn it was not as good as you had hoped, thought, or felt. But that feedback can give you insights that can—and must be—added to your story.

Every session, whether good or horrible, is a unique opportunity to learn. People tend to review a session but forget to write down the learnings. They also tend to beat themselves up for the mistakes they made during that session. It's a waste of time, as we can't change anything—it's in the past.

While it's fresh, while you can feel the hype or the burn, take notes, providing as much detail as possible, not short sentences: What happened? What should have happened? What needs to be changed for the next session? If possible, ask someone to take notes during the session for you; it might be helpful to see how others see your meeting handled.

Keep a list of your mistakes and revisit the list when you start working on your next project. You are allowed to f*ck up once—not twice. We have a tendency to forget, to repeat the same mistake over and over. I record my workshops, for example, and extract the good and the bad. Write your mistakes down, ensure you do not make them again.

A/B test everything if possible. Not sure about something? Test it. Try two options—take the one that out-performed and keep testing the next point. Do not change everything at once, or it will be impossible to know which change was the right one.

Don't overthink it

There is no perfect answer. Take the shot and hope you don't miss. In my experience, many founders tend to overthink things, avoiding decision-making and thus delaying the next actions that must be taken. Making a decision is better than standing still. This is really apparent when choosing your "what" and "how." If you feel decision-making is a problem, cap everything with deadlines, then shorten that deadline by half. Most of the time, we do not need more time. We already know—we made the decision—it is the acting on it that's hard on us. Decide and move forward. Making a bad decision is usually far better than not making that decision. For me, it was one of the hardest lessons to learn and even harder to implement. Improve on the go rather than hoping for constant certainty. Being uncomfortable brings growth, while the cost of moving slowly might mean not moving at all.

It doesn't matter

When asked a while back in an interview if I could share one tip with entrepreneurs, my message was *it doesn't matter.* I mean it in the best possible way. We panic about the meeting, the budget, the client. I was like that for years—but it doesn't matter.

What matters is to keep working hard and give it our best. There will be another pitch. There is always another investor. Everything takes time; some things take more time. Some things we can hurry, while others require patience. It is a long game. A deal that didn't close just now might come back if you think about everything as pieces of this one game, *your* game.

One client goes, another appears. True, I might have made a hundred calls, but sitting at the office horrified about the one that got away will not help. Money comes and goes; so do clients and ideas. We must focus on how we react to the situation at hand, be practical, take a breath, understand what needs to be done, and solve problems.

Journaling

Journaling will instill a habit of writing in you, and it will turn you into your own life's storyteller. It will follow your journey in a way that allows you to revisit your life and the people you have met, but the most important thing is the habit.

Without writing habits, it will be difficult for you to approach the pitch from a writer's perspective. Journaling can help you translate your thoughts and feelings onto paper, give you a fresh look at things, learn how each of these looks on paper. Learn the difference between what you wanted to share and how you tell it; collect and save this journey you are on. You will miss not having it all written—the good, the bad, and the ugly. Many changes made to this book came while journaling my workshop journeys, alone, writing. Only when I read them again did I notice a breakthrough in my thinking, one that made it into the book or workshops. Ten minutes a day, talking to yourself on paper. Writing will become natural for you, not just something you MUST do when pitching.

15

A FINAL WORD

Viva Mexico

Creating a story is so powerful that it can alter our thoughts, beliefs, and even the way we taste things. Let's replace the slides with something else—like a cocktail. Mixology, a fancy name used by bartenders, refers to the art or skill of mixing complex cocktails. It entails so much more than just mixing drinks; it requires an ability to tell the story behind that cocktail.

I was once invited to give a workshop preparing the best bartenders in Israel for the Patron Tequila finals, where each bartender gets to pitch two cocktails, each with its own unique story. *F*ck the Slides* had to deal with tequila cocktails instead of slides. During the competition, 40% of the points were given to the raconteur, the storyteller, the bartender. More than the drink, the garnish, the ingredients, or the taste, the story plays the most significant part. Just like the startup founders, the bartenders put the emphasis on the drinks instead of on writing their story. Most had notes of what they would say, but they never understood the power of controlling the audience. Using experiences and feelings to enhance memories and tastes, we turned those drinks into passionate stories, taking the judges on a journey around the world, through history, places, smells, and tastes. I was so proud of the contestants for working hard, proving a good story can make everything taste and look better.

A few days had passed, and I got on a call with the winner to congratulate her. As she was thanking me, I offered her a few hours of my time because it would bring me pride to say I had worked with a world champion. She was ready to put in the work, test, and improve—and when it came to her craft, she knew what she was doing. I felt a good, unique story could only amplify her cocktails. A few months later, she became the Patron Tequila world champion, winning against 19 other bartenders from around the world.

The story is the spine: it binds it all together, not only the looks but also smells and tastes.

You've got this

We have challenged the status quo. We have proved it can be done differently, and you are now holding the blueprint. The blank canvas will always be the writer's biggest enemy. When, like an addict, you find yourself going back to hiding behind slides, back to improvising, ask yourself, *Why am I hurting my chances of success? How can I craft a story?*

They came for the story, so give them one they will relate to; they will feel, engage, and connect. A good story will make them want more from you. The power to create new worlds, to sell ideas and dreams is completely up to you, within your grasp. You have all the information; you know how to control the audience. You have a powerful ability to create stories and control the narrative. Be confident—you know what you are talking about. When you believe in yourself, the rest is just a process.

Start NOW

Start *now*, not tomorrow, not when you have an important pitch for investors. Start today. You can work on the last sales pitch you had and craft that, or you can prepare for your next meeting, no matter how irrelevant it might be. Put your ideas through the method every time. Treat it just like going to the gym: turn it into a habit. *Practice.* Measure and test as much as you possibly can. Start with some notes before every meeting; set a goal and aim for that. Whenever you pitch, no matter what the purpose will be, the first thing you should do is write it down. You will gain control of the message; you will feel confident, and guessing or self-doubt will disappear. Start small, build from there.

You need less, not more to get your pitch to a final version, and there is never a perfect pitch, just constant improvement, so keep iterating, fixing, asking, and trying until you nail it. The better your foundation is, the better your show will get. Then, and only then, focus on design and everything else, not before.

I wrote this book with the hope of reaching as many people as I can. What started as an idea turned into a talk, which expanded to a workshop. Now, this book should allow you to practice without me by your side. This book isn't designed for the shelf; it was designed for the desk. It is intended to be used often. Keep it close. Revisit the chapters before you pitch, remind yourself to fix a couple of small things each time. Keep tweaking your craft using this book. Practice as much as you possibly can. It will be worthwhile.

One final story

When it comes to naming our projects, we all tend to lose it. Founders can dwell for months, debating names, short lists, and funny variations, crying over names they wanted but are taken. Some brand names are iconic, and some really suck but the companies are doing phenomenally well. For me, as with my book titles and my agency, Streetwise, it is about finding a name and building everything around it. But this time, it was a bit different. I felt *F*ck the Slides*, while a great book title, wouldn't be a good name for a SaaS platform, but what's in a name?

It was the last days of summer. The sun was setting over the Tel Aviv boardwalk. My run was tough; it was hot, humid, but I kept on past the usual stopping point. My mind was occupied, trying to figure out so many things—the main one being that I still didn't have a name for my new platform and it was days from launching. I was in search of something else, an easy name, one word that I would love, that would mean something but was still easy to search online. It was just past the ten-kilometer mark when the idea hit me. I halted, took my phone out, and checked online. The name was available.

Stook. It was a combination of "story" and "hook." But it is also an actual word. "Stook" means a stack of sheaves of grain (or the action of stacking them). Reading this, for the first time in my life, something clicked; the world made sense.

Since childhood, everyone has called me by my surname, almost never by my first name. Zavaro has a nice ring to it, it is unique, whereas Nir is a common name. I have never really cared for it, and traveling and meeting people always meant having to explain it: "No, not Neil, Nir. Like near and far? Yeah, but with an I … oh, never mind, yeah Neil is fine."

I would always joke that I've never had my name right on a coffee cup from Starbucks. But at this moment, my given name made sense. In Hebrew, *Nir* means "harvested field."

It's been over twenty years of hard work, sowing the seeds that would become my passion, crafting my skill, and here it was: after you harvest the field, you get a stook that will serve others.

As my mother always says, everything happens for a reason— and as I always say, everything can be turned into a good story.

And as for you?

You are already a storyteller.

Now, go and be an epic one.

About the Author

Nir Zavaro is an entrepreneur, author, and speaker. He regularly tours the world, on a mission to help as many people as possible become better storytellers. Using his experience, storytelling fundamentals and methods, he brings a fresh perspective on how to implement these into businesses, working with founders and CEOs in over 30 countries.

After a career in the retail industry serving in various roles, Nir founded Streetwise—Creative Sales Agency, specializing in outsourced marketing services. Founded in 2011, the company has worked with hundreds of brands.

Teaching is a major part of his passion, since 2014, he has been a resident lecturer in leading universities and colleges teaching regular courses about branding, marketing and new venture creation, where F*ck the slides was taught. He gives his time mentoring in several hubs and accelerators, helping companies improve their story, brand messaging, pitch decks, and marketing tactics. With two novels under his belt this is his third book and the plan is to keep publishing many more, both novels and management books.

Nir has been involved in several businesses, from online to partner in several successful food and beverage businesses, and today he sits on the advisory board for startups, supporting their brand and marketing efforts.

A member of the Entrepreneurs' Organization (EO), he served on the European Regional Council since 2017, helping launch various marketing initiatives. A fun fact most people do not know, Nir is a former sports channel commentator with three seasons presenting IndyCar racing, three winter Olympics as the Luge, Skeleton and Bobsleigh commentator and even Formula One).

Join Nir's journey:

Website: Nirzavaro.com
Email: zavaro@zavaroness.com
Instagram: nzavaro
Linkedin: nir zavaro

Offer

Sign up for my storyletter: nirzavaro.com

Ready to start your journey? Join the STOOK platform—helping entrepreneurs collect, create, design, and share their stories and presentations. The Stook platform will support you as you master the art of creating compelling stories. Create, measure, practice, share—everything in one place.

Stook.app

Acknowledgments

Years ago, I made a T-shirt riffing on my surname, Zavaro. It said: "*Zavaroness*—A feeling, a state of mind. A contagious sense you can accomplish anything."

A childhood friend told me I couldn't walk around with a T-shirt with my name on it, to which I replied, "But it's ok for you to walk around in underwear with another man's name on it?"

Freedom, for me, is the ability to pursue my dreams. Success is the good fortune of pursuing my dreams surrounded by people who are there for me, helping, pushing, dreaming with me, rooting for me. You can do whatever you want in this world, as long as you surround yourself with people who are willing to support your dreams no matter how insane or farfetched they might sound.

Looking around, I see many who have believed in me. The following is a small list of those who have helped me over the years. I applaud you all.

Shmulik Weiss—you have probably done more for me than anyone. My only hope is that I will be able to repay you. I believe in you, your potential. I hope you will live your dreams every day, no matter what they might be.

Meir Amzalleg—you are a unique individual, a force of nature, able to move hundreds of people around the world during war and scale companies single-handedly, where others needed millions. More than anything, I'm proud to call you my friend. Thank you for everything.

Dan Arav—you are an inspiration when it comes to thirst for learning. A teacher and mentor to me, you make me feel honored to call you a friend. Thank you for opening the door and inviting me to be part of your faculty.

Drinking Tuesday gang—for the company, great stories, amazing food, and endless laughs. Eran Heffetz, Uri Rottenberg—I salute you.

My EO Forum—Zohar Shmueli, Aviv Grafi, Dan Avidar, Dalit Elad, Sharel Omer, and Lana Zaher. Without your pushing and your conviction, the first draft would never have seen the light of day.

The Streetwise crew—my company, my team, my gang. You have all played a part in this journey. I thank you from the bottom of my heart for supporting me all these years. Thank you, Noam Shirman, Gal Attar, Amit Anava, Amit Omer, Inbal

Manor, Guy Rotter, and many more for allowing me to build my dreams together with you.

My parents—I love you. Your endless support and patience never stops amazing me. I'm more thankful than words could describe.

Tomer Zakai—for the book cover, for the style, for being my running buddy, for being so different. You carry yourself in the world like a magical beast of style. I learn so much from you. Thank you.

May Levin—you are tenacious, inspiring. Seeing you conquer so many obstacles reminds me I can always do a little more, do better. I have met many people along the way, and few have your abilities. Thank you for being there for me.

Moran Itzhaki—helping you helped me more than you could ever imagine, and for that I will be forever grateful. You have reminded me that we can have a huge impact on the people we meet along the way.

Dori Tzidon—you crazy guy; the forever kid in you is inspiring. Spending a writing weekend at your place in Serbia will go down as one of my best writing experiences ever.

Leonidas Karellis—storytelling and Greeks; I can't ask for much more, my friend. You are my accountability buddy. I hope we keep pushing each other for years to come.

Dor Bibi—thank you for being a friend, for your patience, for designing our websites and materials, and for supporting me for years.

Raechel Boyko—thank you for your support and encouragement. You play a significant role in my global visibility. Working with you has been a privilege.

Dave Burnett—you are the Canadian Superman. I will never forget what you have done for me. Thank you for being my friend from the other side of the world, reading, reviewing, making this book better.

To Istanbul—the last leg of the book editing. Kishore Mordani, you are an inspiration. Haluk Can Hur and Ayse Inal for hosting me; I am forever grateful for the hospitality.

My EO Tribe—who would believe that joining an organization of like-minded people would result in finding my life's passion. Thanks to all those who took part, who helped me travel the world to serve other entrepreneurs, and thanks for allowing me to go crazy with my ideas and succeed with you all. Thank you, Paul Meester, Myrna Rodriguez, Maria Gergova-bengtsson, Robert van der Zwart, Shen Loong Yen, James Burchell, Brian Keegan, and everyone who took part in this magical journey. Thank you for inviting me into your homes.

Lastly, I want to thank the thousands of people I have met over the years, students, colleagues, founders, and entrepreneurs around the world. Each one of you has given me something to pass along to help someone else along their journey.

Thank you.

Stay authentic, stay true to yourself. Do good, make others feel something; feel comfortable, inspired, intrigued, happy. Make them feel that certain something, that gut feeling that they can trust you. Make them feel they would like to be part of your journey, your story.

If you can make people feel that, my friend, you have won.

Cover Copy

Have you ever sat through a pitch where the presenter read word for word off the slides and thought to yourself, *I could have read through this rubbish at home and done it much quicker?* Have you ever been the presenter reading through the slides word for word and seen the glazed looks from the people who you need to impress to raise your capital or get your project across the line?

Nir Zavaro has been both. F*ck the Slides is a methodology that teaches you how to breathe life, energy, and engagement into every presentation or pitch by mastering the art of storytelling and creating a story so powerful that people can't wait to join your cause.

Say goodbye to leaning on slides. Say hello to nailing every presentation or pitch, no matter what the audience.

Notes

Made in United States
Troutdale, OR
11/03/2023

14281416R00116